The Junior League of Philadelphia's

BICENTENNIAL

COOKBOOK

Photographs by
John T. Chew, Jr.

Chilton Book Company
Radnor, Pennsylvania

Library of Congress Catalog Card Number   75-24997

BICENTENNIAL COOKBOOK

Foreword

I F you have reached the stage in your cooking career where foods are uninteresting and the preparation of another meal is tedious, have heart! Here is a new collection of recipes—some innovative, some heretofore carefully guarded secrets, and some with documented origins. All are from a myriad of forgotten sources and kitchens. Each menu will stimulate your family and guests, simultaneously rekindling your desire to be creative in the kitchen.

All of the recipes were contributed by members of the Junior League of Philadelphia and each one has been tested twice by the committee and its hardworking friends—first as single recipes, then in final menu form. The recipes have been arranged in menus and divided into eight categories. Each is designed to balance and complement the other, please the eye and the palate, and make entertaining easier and more exciting for the chef.

The menus have been set in an historical framework coinciding with the Bicentennial celebration taking place in Philadelphia and throughout the eastern United States. The Philadelphia League covers an eight-county area; from each county a Revolutionary home has been selected to illustrate different types of Colonial architecture and lifestyle. Introducing each section are handsome photographs and information describing these landmarks.

v

Acknowledgments

THE cookbook committee extends sincere thanks and appreciation to each active and sustaining member of the Philadelphia League who contributed her time and interest toward the preparation and publication of this cookbook. We are also grateful to the curators of each house who made it possible for the League to photograph and research each Colonial establishment.

Without the assistance of the following individuals, this book would not be a reality:

Mrs. John S. Bevan
Mrs. Richard A. Brown
Mrs. Nicholas J. Christos
Mrs. John W. Duckett
Mrs. Thomas A. Fernley, III
Mrs. Vincent Fiordalis, II
Mrs. C. Eric Giesa
Mrs. R. Ford Hutchinson
Mrs. J. N. Pattison, IV
Mrs. Peter M. Ramsey
Mrs. William E. Rapp
Mrs. Herbert T. Rorer
Mrs. E. William Ross
Mrs. L. Clark Tierney
Mrs. O. DeGray Vanderbilt, Jr.
Mrs. Theodore Widing, Jr.

Conrad Wilson
  Brinton 1704 House
Mrs. Franklin A. Fleece
  Powel House
Mrs. James I. Wendell
  Pottsgrove Mansion
C. David Murtagh
  John Chads House
Raymond V. Shepherd, Jr.
  Cliveden
Mrs. Marion E. Blaetz
  Mt. Holly Quaker Meeting House
Horace Willcox
  Valley Forge
Wilmer Fisher
  Thompson–Neely House
The Tredyffrin Public Library
The Historical Society of Pennsylvania
The Library Company of Philadelphia

The royalties received from the sale of this cookbook will be returned to the community through the Community Trust Fund of the Junior League of Philadelphia.

Contents

Thompson-Neely House:
Authentic Holiday Celebrations, 187

The purpose of the Junior League is to promote voluntarism; to develop the potential of its members for voluntary participation in community affairs; and to demonstrate the effectiveness of trained volunteers.

The Free Quaker Meeting House, Fifth and Arch Streets, has been the headquarters for The Junior League of Philadelphia since 1969. This small, plain brick building was the meeting house for the Free Quakers who supported the new country by paying taxes to finance the war, and joining the army. The Philadelphia League maintains the building and leases it from the Commonwealth of Pennsylvania.

BRINTON 1704 HOUSE:
Breaking the Fast

Southern face of the Brinton 1704 House,
a quarter mile south of Dilworthtown, Pennsylvania

THE 1704 House built by William Brinton, the younger, is an excellent example of the Colonial farmhouse. It is located in Birmingham Township, Delaware County, Pennsylvania, a quarter of a mile south of Dilworthtown on the old West Chester–Wilmington Pike. The original patent for the land in 1686, conveyed by William Penn's representative to William Brinton, the older, was for four hundred acres of land—which he increased through acquisition to about one thousand acres.

William Brinton (1670–1751), the builder of this home, was the only surviving son of William and Ann Brinton. He married Jane Thatcher in the Birmingham Friends Meeting House. They had six children: four sons and two daughters. And it was for this growing family that the stone house was built.

The home then passed to son Edward and grandson George. During the Battle of Brandywine, September 11–16, 1777, the house and farms were ravaged by the British under "Sir William Howe, K. B. Suporter of Tyranny." They ran ramrods into the cellar floor searching for hidden things of value. The Brintons petitioned for relief in 1782, claiming 1119 pounds, 13 shillings, 1 penny in damages. General Howe said that he would hang the marauders.

The architecture of the Pennsylvania farmhouse was closely related to the Pennsylvania manor house. They were both boldly built and detailed, usually constructed of masonry. In this case, the house was built of stone taken from a nearby quarry. The walls are twenty-two inches thick. There is a steep roof and pent eaves over the first floor windows on the north and south sides of the house. The windows are twenty-seven in number and are of leaded sash. Most of the original floor is still in use.

The basement kitchen was probably the most lived-in room of the house. Cooking was done in front of the oven. Horses were required to bring in logs for the huge fireplaces. Family bread was baked in the beehive oven, which was built within the walls of the house. It had no flue connecting to the chimney, the open door serving this purpose. A fire was made in the oven and when the temperature was sufficiently high, the embers were pulled out into the fireplace, the baking put in the oven and the opening closed with a board.

In the farming community, there was an equality between master and servant. All ate at the same table: in this case, a stretcher table with walnut wainscot chairs. There was a smaller stretcher table along the south wall for the younger members of the family.

Although farm food was not varied, it could almost entirely sustain the household. Articles of luxury had to be imported. The usual Colonial breakfast was milk with bread or hasty pudding, stewed pumpkin, baked apples, and berries as variations. In winter, sweetened cider diluted with water was used. Children enjoyed cider-soaked bread. They were also fed milk pottage, water gruel, flummery, and similar "spoon-meat" or brown bread with cheese.

Basement kitchen of the Brinton House

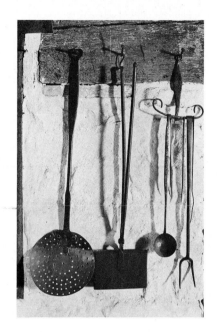

Typical fireplace utensils
in an
eighteenth-century home

Eighteenth-century
stretcher table
set for breakfast

Variety Eggs

8 eggs
¼–½ cup light cream

Break eggs into deep bowl, add cream, and beat until frothy and light. Cook to desired doneness.

Additions: sour cream, chives, substitute ½ vermouth for cream, or melt 3 oz. cream cheese, season with salt and pepper, and add to eggs.

Scrapple

2 cups pork
1½ tsp. salt
⅛ tsp. sage
⅛ tsp. marjoram
½ tsp. pepper
2 cups cornmeal
2 cups whole wheat flour

Boil pork in 4 qt. water. Drain, reserving 3 qt. of the broth. Grind the meat very fine. Bring broth to boil and add the seasonings. Mix cornmeal and flour and add to boiling broth. Add meat. Cook slowly for 30 minutes, stirring frequently. Pour into loaf pans and chill. Slice and fry until brown.

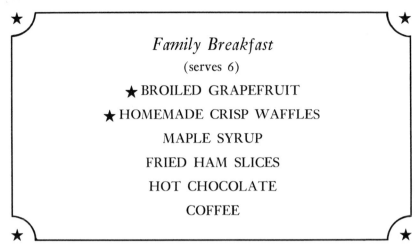

Family Breakfast
(serves 6)

★ BROILED GRAPEFRUIT

★ HOMEMADE CRISP WAFFLES

MAPLE SYRUP

FRIED HAM SLICES

HOT CHOCOLATE

COFFEE

Broiled Grapefruit

Spoon 1 tbsp. of grenadine onto each pink grapefruit half. Sprinkle with brown sugar. Place maraschino cherry on each center. Place under broiler until golden.

Homemade Crisp Waffles

½ lb. butter
2 cups flour
½ tsp. salt
3 tsp. baking powder
1¾ cups milk
2 eggs, separated

Sift all dry ingredients together into mixing bowl. Add egg yolks and milk; beat well. Add melted butter, which has cooled, and beat in. Beat egg whites until stiff and fold in. Bake in waffle iron.

Serve with butter, strawberry jam, or confectioners' sugar.

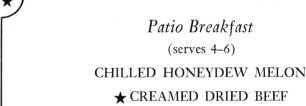

Patio Breakfast
(serves 4–6)

CHILLED HONEYDEW MELON

★ CREAMED DRIED BEEF

★ BAKED HOMINY

★ QUINCE HONEY

★ HONEY WHOLE WHEAT BREAD

Creamed Dried Beef

6 pieces of bacon
2 tbsp. butter or margarine
two 4-oz. packages dried beef
2 tbsp. flour
1½ cups milk
3 hard-boiled eggs, quartered
2 tomatoes, quartered
pepper

Fry the bacon. Remove from pan and drain on paper towel. Pour off fat and put 2 tbsp. butter or margarine in pan. Sauté dried beef. Sprinkle flour over beef and add milk. Stir and fold in eggs and tomatoes. Season with pepper. Serve alongside baked hominy, with bacon on top.

Baked Hominy

¾ cup dried hominy grits
1 tsp. salt
1 cup boiling water
¼ cup butter
1 tbsp. sugar
1 egg, slightly beaten
2 cups milk

Mix water and salt, gradually add hominy, and stir constantly. Bring to boil and boil 2 minutes. Cook in double boiler until water is absorbed. Add 1 cup milk, stirring thoroughly. Cook 1 hour in double boiler.

Remove from heat. Add butter, sugar, egg, and remaining milk. Turn
into buttered casserole dish and bake 1 hour at 325° F.

Quince Honey

5 quince apples
5 lb. sugar
1 pt. water
yellow food coloring

Peel and grate 5 quince apples. Place the apples in a large pot with
1 pt. of water and 5 lb. of sugar. Simmer the ingredients. After boiling
20 minutes or until clear, skim off the foam and add several drops
of food coloring. Place in jars which have been washed and sterilized.
Seal and cool at room temperature.

Honey Whole Wheat Bread

4 cups milk, scalded
¼ lb. margarine
½ cup honey
½ cup dark brown sugar
4 tsp. salt
2 packages dry yeast or 2 cakes compressed yeast
½ cup lukewarm water (about 95° F.)
About 4 lb. stone ground whole wheat flour (Elam's is good)

Combine first 5 ingredients in large mixing bowl. Mix well and cool
to lukewarm. Dissolve yeast in water (adding 1 tsp. of sugar will
speed up the dissolving as you stir). Stir into the milk mixture. Gradually stir in flour as needed to make a stiff dough. (A wooden spoon
is good for this). Beat well after each addition.

Cover bowl with damp tea towel. Let rise in warm, draftfree
place until doubled in bulk; punch down. Knead dough on board
or pastry cloth lightly sprinkled with the flour, until smooth and elastic. Divide into 4 parts for small loaves; 3 parts for large loaves. Shape
into loaves and place in greased loaf pans. Let rise until double in size.
Bake in 375° F oven until done—about 40 minutes to 50 minutes if you
like it crusty.

Remove from pans and cool on wire racks. This bread is made
with natural stone ground whole wheat flour which has no preservative
in it, so it should be refrigerated if it is necessary to keep it a while.
It makes good toast, as well as being delicious plain with butter or
for sandwiches.

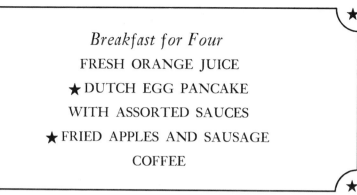

Breakfast for Four

FRESH ORANGE JUICE

★ DUTCH EGG PANCAKE

WITH ASSORTED SAUCES

★ FRIED APPLES AND SAUSAGE

COFFEE

Dutch Egg Pancake

2 tbsp. butter
3 eggs
½ cup flour
½ cup milk
½ tsp. salt

Heat oven at 425° F. Melt butter in heavy 10″ skillet in oven. Beat eggs vigorously for 30 seconds. Gradually beat in flour. Mix in milk and salt. Tip heated pan to coat with butter. Pour in batter, bake 20 minutes. Lower temperature to 300° F and bake 5 minutes.

Cut into wedges: serve with sour cream and brown sugar, lemon butter, assorted syrups, or with melted butter.

Fried Apples and Sausage

1½ lb. small link sausage
4 red apples
bacon drippings

Parboil sausage, then sauté until brown. Core and slice apples. Melt small amount of bacon drippings in frying pan. Sprinkle apples with brown sugar and sauté on both sides.

★

Breakfast for a Group
(serves 8)

BLUEBERRIES AND CREAM

★ PUFFED EGGS

CANADIAN BACON

★ SOUR CREAM COFFEE CAKE

POPOVERS AND ★ CRABAPPLE JAM

★

Puffed Eggs

10 eggs, separated
1 cup sour cream
1 tsp. salt
4 tbsp. butter
grated cheddar cheese

Beat yolks until thick. Beat in sour cream and salt. Beat whites until thick—not dry. Fold whites into yolks. Melt butter in a soufflé dish in the oven. Pour mixture into dish. Put grated cheese on top. Bake 20 minutes at 325° F.

Sour Cream Coffee Cake

½ cup margarine
1 cup sugar
½ pt. sour cream
2 eggs
1 tsp. vanilla
2 cups flour
1 tsp. salt
1 tsp. baking soda
½ tsp. baking powder

Topping
½ cup sugar
1 tsp. cinnamon
½ cup chopped nuts

Cream together ½ cup margarine, 1 cup sugar, sour cream, eggs, and vanilla. Add flour, baking soda, salt, and baking powder.

In a separate bowl, mix together the topping ingredients: sugar, cinnamon, and nuts.

Grease and flour a tube pan or 9" × 13" pan. Add half the batter, half the topping, then remaining batter and topping. Bake at 350° F for 40–45 minutes.

Crabapple Jam

> 5 lb. crabapples (common variety you find flowering in your yard)
> 3½ lb. sugar
> pectin (one box of Sure-Jell or ½ bottle of liquid pectin)
> 5 cups water
> red food coloring

Pick the apples from the tree when they are red and ripe. These are very small apples and you will have to measure them after peeling them. Cut into quarters and place in a large pot with 5 cups of water and simmer for about 10 minutes. Put through a food mill. Place juice back in cleaned pan and add the pectin. Bring to a hard boil, stirring occasionally. Add sugar and bring to a rolling boil (a boil you cannot stir down). Boil for 1 more minute and remove from heat. Add several drops of food color. Skim foam and pour into sterilized jars.

POWEL HOUSE:
Brunch with Distinguished Guests

Exterior of the Powel House, Philadelphia, built in 1765

SAMUEL POWEL, the "patriot mayor," was the last mayor of Philadelphia under the British Crown, and its first high official as a republic. Powel was an arbiter of elegance; he had traveled widely in Europe and was something of a connoisseur and *bon vivant*, delighting in both the pleasures of the table and good company. His wife, Elizabeth Willing Powel (1742–1830) was the nation's first "hostess with the mostest."

The home of Samuel and Elizabeth Powel was a townhouse built in 1765. It has impressive paneled doors of solid mahogany, exquisitely carved mantles above generous fireplaces, multipaned windows, a high ceiling decorated with plaster designs, and a handsomely balustraded stairway. In the courtyard there are embellished walls and alleys filled with boxwood.

The receptions within this house were unrivaled in elegance. The distinguished guest lists were always impressive: General Washington, who later became the first President; the Marquis de Lafayette; foreign ministers. Persons of importance in the colony and nation dined frequently at the Powel table.

One of the notable guests, John Adams, who enjoyed writing about anything that tickled his palate, made the following entry in his diary:

> Dined at Mr. Powells, with Mr. Duché, Dr. Morgan, Dr. Steptoe, Mr. Goldsborough, Mr. Johnson and many others.—A most sinfull Feast again! Every Thing which could delight the Eye, or allure the Taste, Curds and Creams, Jellies, Sweet meats of various sorts, 20 sorts of Tarts, fools, Trifles, floating Island, whipped Sillabubs etc. etc.—Parmesan Cheese, Punch, Wine, Porter, Beer etc. etc.

Obviously, the Powel household sustained Philadelphia's reputation for fine living.

Table setting features French soup plates and tureen c. 1789

Goblet c. 1800 with
P monogram on the
mahogany dining room
table in the
Powel House

Glass case encloses
Sheffield decanter coasters c. 1790
and beakers c. 1800;
Waterford sugar bowl c. 1794;
silver knife and spoon

One of a pair of mahogany
and silver knifeboxes
owned by the Powel family
and made in London c. 1790

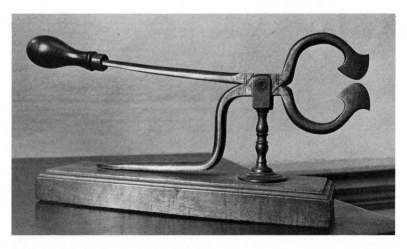

Sugar loaf nipper, wrought steel c. 1770,
used by the Powel family's servants

Marble fireplace in Powel House dining room

South entrance to
Powel House

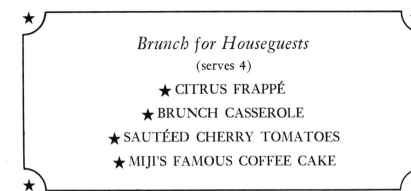

Brunch for Houseguests
(serves 4)

★ CITRUS FRAPPÉ

★ BRUNCH CASSEROLE

★ SAUTÉED CHERRY TOMATOES

★ MIJI'S FAMOUS COFFEE CAKE

Citrus Frappé

½ cup orange juice
¼ cup lemon juice
½ tsp. grated lemon rind
1 cup lemon sherbet
10 crushed ice cubes
2 tbsp. dry sherry (optional)

Combine first 3 ingredients in blender. Process at BLEND for 5 seconds. Add sherbet and ice cubes, process at BLEND for 1 minute until frothy. Process again while adding sherry. Serve in parfait or wine glasses immediately.

Brunch Casserole

7 slices buttered bread
1 cup grated cheddar cheese
½ lb. mushrooms, sautéed in butter
½ lb. cooked sausage
2 eggs
1 cup milk
1 tsp. salt
½ tsp. paprika
½ tsp. dry mustard

Line bottom of baking dish with bread (cut in half into triangles—any remaining, cut into cubes). Sprinkle with layers of cheese, sausage, and mushrooms. Combine and beat eggs, milk, salt, paprika, and dry mustard. Pour these ingredients over bread, cheese, sausage, and mushrooms. Bake at 350° F for about 25 minutes.

Sautéed Cherry Tomatoes

2 pt. cherry tomatoes
1 tbsp. salad oil
3 tbsp. butter
¼ cup chopped parsley

Wash tomatoes and remove stems. Heat oil and butter in skillet. Add tomatoes and parsley; sauté only a few minutes to heat through.

Miji's Famous Coffee Cake

1 cup butter (at room temperature)
2 cups sugar
2 eggs
1 cup sour cream
½ tsp. vanilla
2 cups flour
1 tsp. baking powder
¼ tsp. salt

Topping
4 tsp. sugar
1 cup chopped pecans
1 tsp. cinnamon

Preheat oven to 350° F. Cream together butter and sugar until light and fluffy. Beat in eggs, one at a time. Add vanilla. Fold in sour cream. Sift together dry ingredients. Gradually add to egg mixture.

Pour half of batter into a greased and floured tube pan. Sprinkle with three fourths of the combined topping ingredients. Put in rest of batter. Sprinkle top with remaining topping. Bake for approximately 1 hour at 350° F. Allow to cool before removing from pan.

Brunch for Eight

★ HOT CURRIED FRUIT

WAFFLES WITH ★ CREAMED CHICKEN

CELERY STICKS, GREEN AND BLACK OLIVES

★ LEMON BARS

Hot Curried Fruit

1-lb. can sliced peaches
1 can pears
1 can apricots
14-oz. can pineapple chunks
4-oz. jar maraschino cherries
⅓ cup butter
¾ cup brown sugar
2–3 tbsp. curry powder

Drain fruit well; arrange in baking dish. Melt butter, sugar, and curry powder. Spoon over fruit. Bake 45 minutes to 1 hour at 325° F.

Creamed Chicken

5 whole chicken breasts
¾ cup flour
¾ cup butter
3 cups half and half
3 cups chicken stock
salt
freshly ground pepper

Wash chicken breasts. Place in large kettle of cold water, bring to boil, cover, lower heat, and cook until fork tender. Remove from pot and reduce liquid to 3 cups rich chicken stock. Meanwhile, pick meat from bones, cut into small pieces, and set aside.

In top of double boiler placed over direct heat, melt butter until golden brown, add flour, and make a roux. *Slowly add* 6 cups liquid, stirring constantly with wire whisk to avoid lumps until mixture thickens. Put double boiler together and continue simmering sauce over low heat. Add chicken and correct seasoning. Garnish with fresh parsley and sliced pimento.

Lemon Bars

1 cup butter or margarine
½ cup powdered sugar
2 cups flour
½ tsp. salt
4 eggs
6 tbsp. flour
2 cups sugar
6 tbsp. lemon juice
grated rind of 1 lemon
powdered sugar for top

Blend first 4 ingredients and press into 2 greased 8″ × 8″ pans (or equivalent). Bake at 350° F for 20 minutes or until golden.

Combine eggs, flour, sugar, lemon juice, and rind. Beat thoroughly. Spread over warm pastry. Bake at 350° F for 25 minutes. Cool. Sprinkle with powdered sugar and cut into squares.

★ ★

> *Brunch for Twelve*
>
> CANTALOUPE WITH PORT
>
> AND PROSCIUTTO HAM
>
> ★ SUPER SHIRRED EGGS
>
> ★ GRANDMOTHER'S COFFEE CAKE
>
> GARLIC BUTTER TOASTED ENGLISH MUFFINS
>
> COFFEE

★ ★

Super Shirred Eggs

2 dozen eggs
4 cans whole tomatoes
3 tbsp. Gulden's spicy brown mustard
3 tbsp. worcestershire sauce
¾ cup chili sauce
¼ cup catsup
3 tbsp. lemon juice

Preheat oven to 350° F. Drain tomatoes. Cook in heavy iron skillet. Break up tomatoes with wooden spoon and stir in all ingredients except eggs. When all is well blended and bubbling, remove from stove. Add one egg at a time (break egg into a cup first). Use a tablespoon to maneuver eggs so that they are each surrounded and perhaps covered by the sauce. Cook in oven 30–40 minutes, checking several times until whites are firm and the yolks still soft. Serve right from the pan at the table or buffet.

Variation on Super Shirred Eggs: follow directions for making the sauce in the skillet. When the mixture is well blended and almost bubbly, lower the heat, break eggs one at a time, and stir into sauce. When you have added the eggs and they look just right for scrambled eggs, serve immediately.

Grandmother's Coffee Cake

2 cakes yeast or 2 packages dry yeast
1 cup lukewarm milk (use ½ cup if dry yeast is used)
½ cup sugar
1 tsp. salt
2 eggs
½ cup shortening, softened
4½ cups flour, sifted
½ cup butter, melted
¾ cup sugar
1 tsp. cinnamon
white raisins

Put yeast in warm water for 5 minutes (or follow package instructions). Mix together the milk, sugar, and salt. Add the yeast. Mix in the eggs and shortening, and add the flour gradually, first with a spoon, then by hand. When sticking together, set on floured board and knead with palm of hand. Place dough in bowl, cover, and allow to rise until doubled.

Knead again. Cut into walnut-size balls and dip into melted butter. Roll in combined sugar and cinnamon. Place layer of balls in greased tube pan. Sprinkle with raisins. Place second layer in pan. Let rise 45 minutes. Bake 35–40 minutes at 375° F. Variations: coat bottom of pan with brown sugar. Ice the cake with a powdered sugar and water glaze if desired.

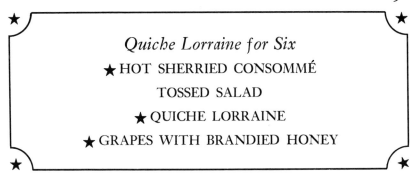

Quiche Lorraine for Six

★ HOT SHERRIED CONSOMMÉ

TOSSED SALAD

★ QUICHE LORRAINE

★ GRAPES WITH BRANDIED HONEY

Hot Sherried Consommé

In a saucepan, heat 2 cans condensed consommé, 1⅓ cups water, and 6 tbsp. dry sherry.

Quiche Lorraine

> short pastry dough for 9″ pie or use prepared crust
> butter
> 1 lb. sliced bacon
> 1 cup grated Swiss cheese
> 4 eggs
> 2 cups light cream
> grated nutmeg
> pinch of salt
> ¾ tsp. salt
> ½ tsp. dry mustard
> pinch of cayenne pepper
> freshly ground pepper

Line pie plate with short pastry dough and rub soft butter over the pastry. Grill bacon until just barely crisp and sprinkle broken pieces over the pastry. Top bacon with grated Swiss cheese; over all, pour mixture of 4 eggs beaten with light cream, a grating of nutmeg, a pinch of sugar, salt, dry mustard, cayenne, and plenty of freshly ground pepper.

Bake at 450° F for 12 minutes then reduce heat to 325° F. Bake until a knife inserted into the center comes out clean (about 25 minutes). Brown slightly under broiler and serve in wedges.

Grapes with Brandied Honey

1 lb. seedless grapes
2 tsp. lemon juice
¼ cup honey
2 tbsp. brandy
½ cup sour cream

Wash and stem grapes. Mix lemon juice, brandy, and honey. Pour over grapes. Let stand overnight. Top each portion with dollops of sour cream. This will keep for several days in refrigerator.

★

Champagne Brunch
(serves 4–6)

CHAMPAGNE PUNCH

STRAWBERRIES AND POWDERED SUGAR

★ CRÊPES WITH CRABMEAT

★ MUSHROOM DELIGHTS

BROILED TOMATOES

★

Crêpes

    1 cup cold milk
    4 eggs
    1 cup water
    1 tbsp. brandy
    ¾ tsp. salt
    2 cups + 1 tsp. sifted flour
    4 tbsp. melted butter or margarine

Put first 4 ingredients into blender. Add flour and butter. Cover and blend at full speed for 1 minute. Scrape mixture off sides of jar and blend a few seconds more. Cover and refrigerate mixture for 2–3 hours. When ready to make crêpes, stir mixture with a spoon (it should be thick enough to coat the spoon). If too thick, add a little water to the batter. Makes 10–12 crêpes.

Crabmeat

    2 cups white sauce
    1 tsp. butter
    7½-oz. can King crabmeat, drained
    1 tsp. chopped shallots or green onions
    ½ cup dry white wine
    ½ tsp. worcestershire sauce
    ⅛ tsp. pepper
    dash of cayenne
    1 recipe crêpes

Separate crabmeat, removing membrane and bones. In medium skillet, sauté shallot or onion in butter one minute. Add crabmeat, Sauté 2 minutes longer. Add wine, worcestershire sauce, pepper, and cayenne. Cook over medium heat, stirring, for 3 minutes. Stir in 1 cup of the white sauce just until blended. Use the other cup of white sauce to spoon on top of the crepes after filling.

Mushroom Delights

1 lb. large fresh mushrooms
2 tbsp. butter or margarine
2 tbsp. chopped onion
¾ oz. sharp cheddar cheese, American or Parmesan
Approximately 2 tbsp. seasoned (preferably Italian)
     breadcrumbs

Wash mushrooms and drain. Remove stems and place caps in baking dish. Chop stems finely. Melt butter, sauté onion in it, then add stems and cheese. Cook over low heat until liquid is absorbed. Thicken mixture with seasoned breadcrumbs until paste-like. Stuff caps with mixture. Bake in moderate oven for 10 minutes. Serve.

Very large caps may be used as a formal appetizer or side dish with roast. They take longer to cook.

Variation: Add ¼ cup chopped ripe olives.

Cheese Soufflé

1 cup milk (scalded)
2 cups bread cubes
4 tbsp. butter
1 tsp. salt
¼ tsp. pepper
1 tsp. dry mustard
1 cup grated cheese
6 egg yolks and whites (separated)

1919169

Scald milk. Add bread cubes, butter, salt, pepper, and dry mustard. Then add grated cheese. Let cool a bit. Add beaten egg yolks. Beat whites of eggs and fold in carefully. Pour into greased casserole. Bake at 325° F until set, around 25 minutes.

Manhattan Ice

1 cup orange juice
1½ tbsp. lemon juice
½ cup sugar
1 cup heavy cream
¼ cup sugar
⅓ cup chopped nuts, if desired
½ tsp. vanilla

Mix orange juice and lemon juice with ½ cup sugar. Stir until sugar is dissolved; put in refrigerator tray. Whip cream. Beat in ¼ cup sugar. Add nuts and vanilla. Spread carefully over orange juice mixture while still in liquid form. Place in freezer. When firm, slice and serve with a delicate cookie.

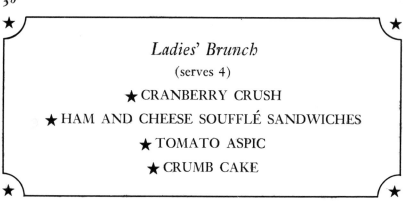

Ladies' Brunch

(serves 4)

★ CRANBERRY CRUSH

★ HAM AND CHEESE SOUFFLÉ SANDWICHES

★ TOMATO ASPIC

★ CRUMB CAKE

Cranberry Crush

whiskey or rum
whiskey sour mix
cranberry juice

Combine all in equal parts. Freeze. Remove and stir until slushy before serving.

Ham and Cheese Soufflé Sandwiches

8 slices bread (homemade is best)
butter
½ lb. cheddar cheese
4 slices ham
2 cups milk
4 eggs
1 tsp. salt
1 tsp. paprika

Cut crusts from bread and spread 1 side of each slice with butter. Place 4 slices, buttered side down, in greased flat pan. Put a slice of ham and cheese on each and cover with other bread—buttered side up. Make a custard of remaining ingredients: beat eggs slightly, add milk, salt, and paprika, and blend well. Pour over sandwiches and refrigerate for several hours or overnight. Bake at 350° F for 45 minutes.

Tomato Aspic

1 tbsp. unflavored gelatin (1 envelope)
2 tbsp. cold water
2 tbsp. boiling water
10½-oz. can tomato soup
2 cups tomato juice
3-oz. package lemon jello
⅛ tsp. salt
1½ tbsp. vinegar
minced onions
ground cloves
watercress

Soak unflavored gelatin in cold water. Dissolve in boiling water. Add can of tomato soup. Heat tomato juice. Dissolve jello in heated tomato juice. Combine 2 mixtures. Add salt, vinegar, minced onions, and a dash of ground cloves. Pour into individual molds and chill. Garnish with watercress.

Crumb Cake

½ cup butter
2 tsp. baking powder
1 cup sugar
2 eggs, separated
½ cup milk
2 cups flour

Sift together flour, sugar, and baking powder. Add butter and crumble well with fingers. Take out ½ cup crumbs. To remaining mix, add well beaten yolks and milk. Fold in stiffly beaten egg whites. Mix well. Pour mixture into well-greased deep pan (9″). Sprinkle top with crumbs. Bake in 350° F oven for 40 minutes. When finished baking, sprinkle top with melted butter and cinnamon.

Company Brunch
(serves 12)

★ SIMPLE BLOODY MARYS

GIN FIZZES

EGGS BENEDICT

★ BUTTERMILK COFFEE CAKE

or

★ DANISH PUFF PASTRY

★ SOUR CREAM FRUIT FLUFF

Simple Bloody Marys

24 oz. vodka
48 oz. Clamato juice
24 oz. V-8 juice
2 tbsp. worcestershire sauce
Tabasco to taste
¾ tsp. salt
¾ tsp. pepper
12 slices lemon

Fill 12 tall glasses with ice and add lemon slices. Pour vodka, Clamato juice, V-8 juice, and worcestershire sauce into a large pitcher. Add Tabasco, salt, and pepper to taste. Stir and fill the glasses.

Buttermilk Coffee Cake

3 cups flour
2 cups sugar
2 tsp. baking soda
2 tsp. cream of tartar
½ tsp. salt
¾ cup Crisco
2 eggs
2 cups buttermilk
¾ cup finely chopped walnuts

Sift together flour, sugar, baking soda, cream of tartar, and salt. Cut in the Crisco. Beat in the eggs, buttermilk, and walnuts. Pour half the batter into a well-greased 13″ × 9″ pan. Sprinkle with cinnamon. Add remaining batter. Sprinkle with brown sugar and cinnamon. Dot with butter.

Bake at 350° F for approximately 1 hour or until knife comes out clean.

Danish Puff Pastry

>2 cups margarine
>2 cups flour
>2 tbsp. cold water
>1 cup boiling water
>1 tsp. almond extract
>3 eggs

Frosting:
>2 cups confectioners sugar
>1 tsp. vanilla
>1 tbsp. margarine
>2–3 tbsp. milk or cream

Cut 1 cup margarine into 1 cup of the flour until it resembles coarse meal. Add 2 tbsp. cold water and stir until well blended. Divide in half. Press each half onto ungreased cookie sheet, shaping into 3″ × 12″ oblong.

In pan, bring to boil 1 cup water and 1 cup margarine. Add 1 tsp. almond extract. Remove from heat and stir in 1 cup flour. Add 3 eggs, *one at a time*, and beat each well. Spread mixture over crust. Bake at 425° F for 50 minutes.

Combine ingredients for frosting and ice pastry while still hot.

Sour Cream Fruit Fluff

>3⅝-oz. package instant vanilla pudding mix
>2 cups cold milk
>1 cup dairy sour cream
>assorted fresh fruit and berries

Pour milk into bowl and add pudding. Beat slowly for 1 to 2 minutes, until well blended. Fold in sour cream. Chill completely. Arrange slices of assorted fresh fruits and berries on platter around bowl full of topping.

POTTSGROVE MANSION:
Leisurely Luncheons

Pottsgrove Mansion, built in 1752 by the Potts family

PENNSYLVANIA is America's Iron State and the Potts family is known as the First Family of Iron. The first iron furnace in Pennsylvania was established by Thomas Potts and Thomas Rutter in 1720 at Colebrookdale. Thomas Potts' son, John (1710–1768), an active pioneer and proprietor, further expanded the family's interest.

In Colonial days, an active home life was insured by the large numbers of children so often produced. John Potts and his wife, Ruth Savage Potts, were fortunate to have thirteen children, several of whom distinguished themselves during the Revolution: Thomas as a member of the State Constitutional Convention in 1776; Jonathan as Director General of Hospitals of the Northern Division of the American Army; and Issac, whose Valley Forge home became Washington's Headquarters during 1777–1778.

The family home, Pottsgrove Mansion, built in 1752 by John Potts, was constructed of fieldstone. The Georgian interior is furnished primarily with Philadelphia Chippendale.

To preserve the comfort and elegance of family meals, the children dined in a separate area. They ate their gruel or milk pottage in silence, as fast as possible (regardless of indigestion), and left the table promptly. Between meals, a child could have dry bread and warm "small beer".

Small Beer

Boil 2 oz. of hops for 3 or 4 hours in 3 or 4 pails full of water. Then scald 2 qt. of molasses in the liquor. Pour boiling mixture into a clean half barrel. Fill the barrel with cold water. Before the barrel is almost full, put in the yeast. The next day, you will have "agreeable wholesome small beer."

Pewter place setting
in the children's
dining room

The children's dining room at Pottsgrove and the furnishings therein
were built to approximately three-quarter scale

Burl bowl on an
early tavern table
in the children's
dining room

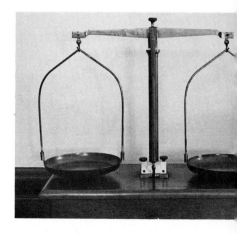

Colonial scales

nnon by North
rance path at
tsgrove Mansion

Looking from the gardens toward
the western face of Pottsgrove

POTTSGROVE

Built in 1752 by John
Potts, ironmaster. Wash-
ington's headquarters
for five days~Sept.1777.

Administered by the Pennsylvania
Historical and Museum Commission

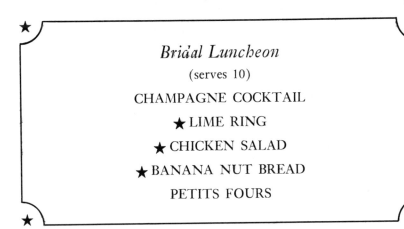

Bridal Luncheon

(serves 10)

CHAMPAGNE COCKTAIL

★ LIME RING

★ CHICKEN SALAD

★ BANANA NUT BREAD

PETITS FOURS

Lime Ring

6-oz. package lime Jello
1 qt. vanilla ice cream
1 large can crushed pineapple (save juice)
1½ cups grated sharp cheese
2 cups juice from pineapple, boiled (using hot water to make
   2 cups if necessary)

Dissolve Jello in hot pineapple juice. Add ice cream and dissolve. Add cheese, then pineapple. Pour into 2-qt. ring mold. Refrigerate. When set, unmold and fill center with chicken salad. Garnish with fresh strawberries.

Chicken Salad

6 whole chicken breasts
1 cup French dressing
mayonnaise
½ cup capers
1 cup chopped celery
onion salt
freshly ground pepper

Wash and split chicken breasts. Place in pan and bake at 350° F until fork tender. Remove meat from bones while still warm and cut into bite-size pieces. Pour favorite French dressing over chicken. Season, toss lightly, cover, and refrigerate. Allow to marinate at least 2 hours.

Before serving, add celery, capers, and mayonnaise. Mix until desired consistency.

Banana Nut Bread

    2½ cups flour
    1 cup sugar
    3½ tsp. baking powder
    1 tsp. salt
    3 tbsp. salad oil
    ¾ cup milk
    1 egg
    1 cup chopped nuts
    1 cup mashed bananas

Measure all ingredients into a bowl. Beat 1 minute, scraping sides of bowl constantly. Place in 9″ × 5″ × 3″ pan (greased and floured). Bake at 350° F for 55–65 minutes. For plain nut bread, increase milk to 1¼ cups and omit bananas.

★ ★

Ladies' Summer Luncheon

(serves 4–6)

★ BEET–CUCUMBER SOUP

★ CRAB CASSEROLE

WATERCRESS AND BIBB LETTUCE

WITH FRENCH DRESSING

BREADSTICKS

★ LEMON LOAF AND FRUIT SHERBERT

★ ★

Beet–Cucumber Soup

2 cups beef stock
1 onion, sliced
1 large cucumber, peeled and sliced
salt, freshly ground pepper, lemon juice
½ cup chilled sour cream
3 raw beets, peeled
cucumber slices
chopped chives

Combine the stock, onion, and cucumber; bring to a boil, and cook 5 minutes. Whirl in the blender until smooth and season with salt and pepper to taste. Grate raw beets, put in a saucepan, and cover with water and salt. Bring to a boil and cook 4–5 minutes. Combine with cucumber mixture and chill. Stir in sour cream. Serve garnished with cucumber slices and chives.

Crab Casserole

¾ lb. mushrooms
5 tbsp. butter
1 tbsp. green onion
1 tbsp. chives
1 tbsp. parsley
3 tbsp. flour
2 cups sour cream
1½ cups crabmeat
3 tbsp. sherry or sauterne
salt and pepper
paprika

Wash and slice mushrooms. Cook stems in enough water to just cover them, for about 5 minutes. Drain and set aside. Heat butter in frying pan and sauté mushrooms. Add onions, chives, parsley; sauté until brown. Add 3 tbsp. flour. Blend well and moisten with 2 cups sour cream and 2 or 3 tbsp. mushroom stock. Season with salt and pepper. Add crab and put in casserole. Put sherry or sauterne on top and sprinkle with paprika. Bake at 350° F for ½ hour.

Lemon Loaf

6 tbsp. margarine
1 cup sugar
1 tsp. baking powder
2 beaten eggs
½ cup milk
1½ cups pecans chopped fine (5½-oz. package)
1½ cups flour
¼ tsp. salt
grated rind of 1 lemon
juice of 2 lemons combined with ⅓ cup sugar

Cream margarine and sugar with electric beater. Add beaten eggs, then milk and rind (the batter will probably look curdled). Sift dry ingredients and blend in quickly. Add nuts. Spoon batter into greased loaf pan. Bake at 350° F for 1 hour and 5 minutes. The second you remove from oven, pour over the lemon juice–sugar mixture.

Children's Birthday Luncheon
★ LUNCH ON AN APPLE

POTATO CHIPS

GRAPE JUICE AND GINGER ALE

★ SNOWDEN CHOCOLATE COOKIES

or

★ HERMIT COOKIES

★ GRAMMY GIRL CAKE

Lunch on an Apple

For each serving, stud an apple with cubes of bologna, American cheese, sweet pickles, cherry tomatoes, pineapple, grapes, miniature marshmallows, etc., on toothpicks.

Snowden Chocolate Cookies

2 cups sugar
1 cup butter
2 eggs
4 squares chocolate, melted
2 tsp. vanilla
4 tsp. milk
2 tsp. baking powder
⅛ tsp. salt
2½ cups flour
½ cup chopped pecans

Cream butter and sugar. Stir in eggs, chocolate, vanilla, and milk. Sift dry ingredients and fold into batter. Add pecans. Drop by teaspoonfuls onto lightly greased cookie sheet. Bake at 300° F for 10 minutes. Makes 5 dozen. Put in bags and give as favors.

Hermit Cookies

½ lb. butter
1½ cups brown sugar
3 eggs, beaten
1 tsp. baking soda
⅓ cup hot water
¼ tsp. salt
3 cups flour
1 tsp. cinnamon
1 lb. seedless raisins
½ lb. walnuts, chopped

Cream butter and sugar; add beaten eggs; dissolve soda in water and add. Sift the flour, cinnamon, and salt, then add them to the mixture along with the raisins and walnuts. Let dough stand in the refrigerator overnight. Pinch off little pieces and place 2″ apart on a greased baking pan. Bake at 350° F for 12 minutes, or until lightly browned. Place on rack to cool. Makes 10 dozen.

Grammy Girl Cake

1 large angel food cake
1 cup sugar
½ lb. butter
4 egg yolks, lightly beaten
juice of 1 lemon
grated rind of 2 lemons
4 egg whites
1 pt. whipping cream (whipped)
2 tsp. sugar
1 tsp. vanilla
½ tsp. almond extract

Slit a large angel food cake horizontally to make 3 layers.

Cream together sugar and butter. Slowly add egg yolks, lemon juice, and rind. Beat egg whites dry and add to batter. Cover the 3 layers and outside of cake with this mixture. Refrigerate overnight. Before serving, ice all over with whipped cream to which the sugar and vanilla and almond extract have been added. Decoration such as colored sugar, candied cherries, or slivered almonds may be added.

Spring Luncheon
(serves 8)
RED AND WHITE COLE SLAW
★ MOLDED SALMON SALAD
★ POPPY SEED BREAD
★ BRANDIED NECTARINES

Molded Salmon Salad

2 envelopes gelatin
½ cup cold water
½ cup boiling water
4 tbsp. sugar
2 tbsp. lemon juice
2 tbsp. vinegar
4 tbsp. grated onion
1 tsp. salt
1 tbsp. horseradish
two 1-lb. cans red salmon: drained, flaked, boned
1 cup mayonnaise
⅔ cup chopped sweet pickles
½ cup chopped celery

Soften the gelatin in the cold water and add to the boiling water. Mix together the rest of the ingredients, then add the gelatin. Spoon into a 6-cup wet mold and chill overnight.

Poppy Seed Bread

2¼-oz. box poppy seeds
1 cup milk
1½ cups sugar
2 cups flour
2½ tsp. baking powder
¼ tsp. salt
½ cup butter
2 eggs, slightly beaten
½ tsp. vanilla

Soak seeds in milk 1 hour. Sift flour, sugar, baking powder, and salt together. Cut in butter until crumbly. Add seeds and milk and mix 2 minutes, until smooth. Add vanilla and eggs and mix 2 additional minutes. Pour into greased and floured loaf pan and bake at 350° F for 1 hour.

Brandied Nectarines

6 nectarines
1 cup sugar
1 cup water
4 tbsp. brandy
1½ tsp. vanilla
½ cup sour cream
2 tbsp. powdered sugar

Cut the nectarines into quarters, combine in pan with sugar and water, and boil for 1 minute. Stir in 3 tbsp. of the brandy and the vanilla. Chill. Combine the sour cream, powdered sugar, and the rest of the brandy. Spoon this mixture over the nectarines just before serving.

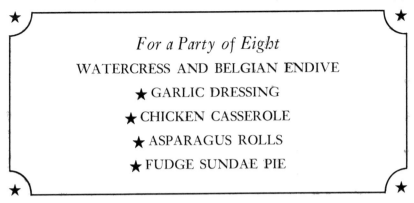

For a Party of Eight

WATERCRESS AND BELGIAN ENDIVE

★ GARLIC DRESSING

★ CHICKEN CASSEROLE

★ ASPARAGUS ROLLS

★ FUDGE SUNDAE PIE

Garlic Dressing

In a blender, put:
2 tbsp. cider vinegar (generous tbsp.)
1 tsp. salt
½ tsp. ground pepper

Turn on blender and add ⅓ cup + 1 tbsp. oil, and 3 or 4 garlic cloves, 2 heaping tbsp. mayonnaise, and 2 heaping tbsp. sour cream. Use immediately.

Chicken Casserole

4 cups cubed, cooked chicken
2 tbsp. lemon juice
¾ cup mayonnaise
1 tsp. salt
2 cups chopped celery
4 hard-boiled eggs, chopped
¾ cup cream of chicken soup
1 tsp. minced onion
⅔ cup almonds
1 cup potato sticks
1 cup grated cheese

Combine all ingredients except the last three. Place in a casserole, and top with the almonds, potato sticks, and cheese. Place in refrigerator overnight. Bring to room temperature before heating. Bake at 400° F for 20–25 minutes, until heated through.

Asparagus Rolls

soft, thin-sliced bread
mayonnaise
whipped cream cheese
bleu cheese spread
cooked jumbo asparagus spears, fresh or frozen
melted butter

For each roll, trim the crusts from the bread and spread with combined mayonnaise, cream cheese and bleu cheese spread in equal amounts. Roll an asparagus spear in the bread. When ready to serve, brush with melted butter and bake at 350° F for 25 minutes.

Fudge Sundae Pie

1 cup evaporated milk
6-oz. package chocolate chips
1 cup miniature marshmallows
¼ tsp. salt
approximately 30 vanilla wafers
1½ qt. vanilla ice cream, slightly softened
pecan halves

Combine milk, chocolate chips, marshmallows, and salt in top of double boiler over medium heat. Stir until it melts and becomes thickened. Cool. Line bottom and sides of a 9″ pie pan with vanilla wafers. Starting with ice cream, alternate layers with chocolate mixture. Top with pecan halves. Freeze until firm. Let soften slightly before cutting.

Afternoon Tea

(serves 10)

★ SANDWICH LOAF

SALTED NUTS

★ CRANBERRY NUT BREAD

BUTTER MINTS

TEA AND COFFEE

Sandwich Loaf

1 uncut loaf of bread
butter
sandwich fillings: minced ham, egg salad, chopped watercress,
    and mayonnaise
two 8-oz. packages cream cheese, softened with mayonnaise
or:
two 8-oz. packages whipped cream cheese.

Cut the crusts off the bread and slice horizontally three times, forming four even layers. Butter each layer. Fill with above spreads. Assemble the layers and frost with the cream cheese, as you would a cake. Decorate with carrot curls, radish slices, or parsley. *Refrigerate* before serving and cut each piece very thin.

Cranberry Nut Bread

2 cups flour
1 cup sugar
1½ tsp. baking powder
½ tsp. soda
3 tbsp. shortening (melted)
1 cup cranberries, cut in halves
½ cup chopped nuts
1 well-beaten egg
juice from 1 orange and enough water to measure 1 cup

Mix all dry ingredients (except cranberries and nuts). Mix egg, shortening, and diluted orange juice: add gradually to dry ingredients.
Stir slightly until mixed. Add nuts and cranberries. Bake in greased
and floured loaf pan for 1 hour at 350° F (40 minutes for aluminum
pans).

Informal Lunch
(serves 6)

★ CREAM OF TOMATO SOUP

★ GRILLED CLUB SANDWICH

POTATO CHIPS

PICKLES

FRESH PINEAPPLE DIPPED IN POWDERED SUGAR

Cream of Tomato Soup

4 cups buttermilk
2 cans tomato soup
½ tsp. worcestershire sauce
¼ tsp. salt
¼ tsp. Tabasco
1 tbsp. minced onion

Mix buttermilk and soup. Add onion, worcestershire, salt, and Tabasco. Chill. Garnish with lemon slices, fresh basil, or cubed tomatoes.

Grilled Club Sandwich

turkey slices
ham slices
Swiss cheese or American cheese slices
butter
bread slices
1 egg
¾ cup milk

Beat together egg and milk. Butter bread and make sandwiches of turkey, ham, and cheese combination. Butter griddle or pan in preparation to grill sandwiches. With pastry brush, coat both sides of sandwiches with egg and milk mixture. Grill on each side until golden brown.

Tailgate Luncheon

(serves 8–10)

★ HOMEMADE VEGETABLE SOUP

★ COLD FRIED CHICKEN

KAISER ROLLS

★ BANANA CAKE

Homemade Vegetable Soup

4-qt. kettle
1 large soup bone with meat
3 short ribs
1 large turnip, diced
4 large carrots, scraped and diced
½ head cabbage, grated
1 box each: frozen cut green beans, cut yellow wax beans, fordhook lima beans, sweet peas
4 ears fresh corn
1 large can tomatoes, cut into small pieces (undrained)
¼ cup rice, washed
1 onion, sliced
1 rib celery, cut
2 tbsp. salt
1 tbsp. pepper, freshly ground
parsley
Accent
sugar

Place bone and ribs in 4-qt. kettle. Cover with cold water almost to top of pot. Add onion, celery, parsley, and 1 tbsp. salt. Cook until meat is tender. Remove meat from bones and boil down liquid by ¼ only. Strain broth and reserve.

Meanwhile, cook turnips, carrots, and cabbage together in boiling water. Discard liquid when vegetables are fork tender. Cook all frozen vegetables according to package directions and set aside. Scrape corn from ears and cook separately. When all vegetables are cooked and drained, add all ingredients, including rice and tomatoes (undrained), to reserved broth. Simmer over low heat until rice is tender. Season with sugar to taste, salt, pepper, and Accent.

Cold Fried Chicken

split chicken breasts and drumsticks
eggs
milk or light cream
flour for dredging
salt, pepper, paprika, garlic powder
24-oz. bottle oil

Dilute eggs with milk and beat together (use enough to dip all pieces of chicken). Place flour in bag. Season with salt, pepper, paprika, and garlic powder. Dip chicken pieces in egg first, then toss in bag of flour. Heat oil in frying pan to 375° F and place chicken, skin side down, in oil. Cook for 10–12 minutes until golden (slightly longer for legs). Turn and cook about 10 minutes longer. Drain on paper towel.

Banana Cake

¾ cup buttermilk
2 cups sifted cake flour
1 tsp. baking powder
1 tsp. baking soda
½ tsp. salt
½ cup shortening
1½ cups sugar
1 egg, slightly beaten
1 egg yolk, slightly beaten
1 cup mashed bananas
½ cup pecans, finely chopped
1 tsp. vanilla
butter cream icing

Sift and measure flour, then sift in all dry ingredients. Cream shortening and sugar. Add eggs, bananas, and nuts. Add flour and milk alternately to egg mixture. Add vanilla. Pour into three 8″ layer cake pans. Bake at 350° F for 25 minutes. Frost with butter cream icing. Refrigerate.

Quiche for Six

★ SWISS QUICHE

★ HAM SAUCE or CRABMEAT SAUCE

CLOVERLEAF ROLLS

★ HONEY DATE BARS

INTERNATIONAL COFFEE

Swiss Quiche

unbaked 9″ pastry shell
4 eggs, separated
1½ cups light cream
½ tsp. salt
⅛ tsp. ground nutmeg
6 oz. natural Swiss cheese, shredded (1½ cups)

Bake pastry shell at 450° F for 7 minutes. Remove and reduce oven to 350° F. Slightly beat the egg yolks and add the cream, salt, and nutmeg. Beat the egg whites until stiff peaks form. Fold into the egg yolk mixture, then fold in the cheese. Pour into the pastry shell. Bake at 350° F for 40–45 minutes, or until a knife inserted comes out clean. Let stand 5 minutes. Serve with Ham or Crabmeat Sauce.

Crabmeat Sauce

1 cup crabmeat, or 7-oz. can. drained and flaked
2 tbsp. butter
1 tbsp. flour
⅛ tsp. salt
1 cup light cream

Heat the crab in the butter, blend in the flour and salt, then add the cream. Cook and stir until thickened.

Ham Sauce

1 cup ham, diced
2 tbsp. butter
1 tbsp. flour
1 cup light cream

Heat the ham in the butter, blend in the flour, and add the cream.
Cook and stir until thickened.

Honey Date Bars

1 egg
⅓ cup honey, or ½ cup sugar
¼ tsp. baking powder
2½ tbsp. flour
pinch of salt
½ cup dates, stoned and chopped
½ cup chopped nuts

Beat egg until light, add honey or sugar, then baking powder sifted
with flour and salt. Add dates and nuts. Turn into a 6½"-square tin,
lined with waxed paper. Bake at 325° F for 25 minutes. When cool, cut
into strips 2" × ¾". Roll in granulated sugar, pack in a covered container, and keep at least 1 week before using.

★ ★

> ## *Formal Luncheon*
> (serves 8)
>
> ★ CUCUMBER MOUSSE
>
> SLICED TOMATOES AND AVOCADO
>
> ★ CHICKEN IN WINE
>
> ★ RICE TIMBALES
>
> COFFEE ICE CREAM
>
> WITH
>
> ★ CHOCOLATE SAUCE AND TOASTED COCONUT

★ ★

Cucumber Mousse

3-oz. package lime gelatin
¾ cup boiling water
1 package unflavored gelatin
¼ cup cold water
1 cup mayonnaise
1 tbsp. minced onion
1 cup cottage cheese
1 medium cucumber, peeled and chopped
⅛ tsp. Tabasco sauce
1 clove garlic, minced
½ cup slivered almonds
green food coloring

Dissolve lime gelatin in boiling water, then unflavored gelatin in cold water. Put mayonnaise, onion, cottage cheese, cucumber, Tabasco, garlic, and almonds in blender. Blend well, then add lime and unflavored gelatins. Blend again. Add green food coloring for eye appeal. Mold and chill overnight. Serve on lettuce leaves.

Chicken in Wine

3 tbsp. butter
¾ cup chopped onion
4 chicken breasts, split and skinned
2 tbsp. flour
2 tbsp. chopped parsley
1 tsp. marjoram
½ bay leaf
½ tsp. thyme
1 tsp. salt
⅛ tsp. pepper
1 tbsp. brandy
1 large can sliced mushrooms
1½ cups sauterne

Cook onion in butter until transparent. Add chicken and *lightly* brown. Remove chicken and add next 8 ingredients. When well mixed, add mushrooms and wine. Place chicken in casserole and pour sauce over it. May be made early and refrigerated at this point. Bake at 350° F for 1 hour. Serve with rice timbales.

Rice Timbales

Prepare rice according to package directions. Shape into mounds and serve separately.

Chocolate Sauce

2 cups sugar
1 cup evaporated milk
½ lb. unsweetened chocolate
1 tbsp. butter
1 tbsp. vanilla
¼ tsp. salt

Place all ingredients in the top of a double boiler and cook until smooth. Serve over coffee ice cream and sprinkle with toasted coconut.

Finance Committee Lunch

(serves 8)

★ FINANCE COMMITTEE SOUP

★ OPEN-FACE SHRIMP SANDWICHES

★ DEVILED EGGS

RELISH TRAY

★ MUMU'S BROWNIE PIE À LA MODE

Finance Committee Soup

1 large can tomato soup
1 can beef bouillon
2 cans pea soup
curry powder
sherry

Mix together the cans of soup, add half the total amount of water, and heat. Add curry powder and sherry to taste. Garnish with sour cream and chives.

Open-Face Shrimp Sandwiches

two 4-oz. cans small shrimp
1 cup chopped celery
4 tbsp. finely chopped onion
1 cup sharp grated cheese
1 cup mayonnaise
8 slices bread

Toast the bread on one side. Combine the rest of the ingredients. Spread the shrimp mixture on the untoasted side of the bread. Bake at 350° F for 15 minutes.

Deviled Eggs

6 hard-boiled eggs
¼ cup mayonnaise
¼ tsp. worcestershire sauce
1 tbsp. soft butter
¼ tsp. dry mustard
freshly ground pepper, to taste

Halve eggs and remove yolks. Mash with fork or in electric mixer with butter. Add remaining ingredients and beat until smooth. If mixture is too stiff, add more mayonnaise. Fill whites and garnish with parsley and paprika.

MuMu's Brownie Pie

½ lb. butter
5 squares Hershey's unsweetened chocolate
2 cups sugar
1 cup flour, *before* sifting
¼ tsp. baking powder
¼ tsp. salt
1 cup pecans, chopped
4 eggs, beaten
vanilla to taste
French vanilla ice cream

Melt butter and chocolate in top of double boiler. Sift flour, salt, and baking powder. Add sugar to chocolate mixture, stirring well. Fold in beaten eggs. Remove from heat and add flour, vanilla, and nuts. Mix well. Pour into greased 9″ pie plate. Bake at 350° F for 30–35 minutes. Will also make one 9″ × 9″ pan of brownies. Top with scoop of ice cream.

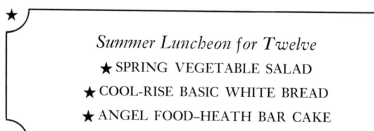

Spring Vegetable Salad

1 bottle oil and vinegar French dressing
3 medium zucchini, sliced thin
½ lb. fresh mushrooms, sliced
1 lb. fresh green beans, trimmed and halved
1 can chick peas, drained
4 carrots, julienne sliced
1 large head leaf lettuce
2 cups cubed cooked chicken, ham, or roast beef
1 box cherry tomatoes
¼ lb. Swiss cheese, julienne sliced

Marinate the fresh vegetables in the French dressing overnight. Rinse the lettuce and place it in a bed in a large salad bowl or platter. Drain the vegetables and reserve the marinade. Toss the chicken in the reserved marinade, then add to the vegetables. Heap this all on the lettuce bed and garnish with cherry tomatoes and Swiss cheese.

Cool-Rise Basic White Bread

2 packages dry yeast
½ cup warm water
2 tbsp. sugar
1¾ cups warm milk
1 tsp. salt
2 tbsp. butter
5½ to 6½ cups sifted flour
oil

Dissolve yeast in warm water, then add the sugar. In a large bowl, place the warm milk, salt, and butter; then add the yeast mix. Add the flour, 1 cup at a time, mixing well. *After 3 or 4 cups have been added, mix well for 2 minutes.* THEN add the remaining flour, *reserving 1 cup for kneading.* Turn onto a floured cloth and let set for 10–15 minutes.

Knead for 5–10 minutes, until smooth and elastic and dough is no longer sticky. Put in greased bowl and cover with a towel. Let stand 20 minutes. Punch down. Divide in half. Form and put into loaf pans. Brush with oil. Refrigerate 2–24 hours. Let stand at room temperature for 10 minutes, then bake at 400° F for 30–40 minutes (375° F for Pyrex pans).

Angel Food–Heath Bar Cake

1 angel food cake
15 Heath Bars, crushed
2 cups heavy cream
1 jar butterscotch sauce

Slice angel food cake horizontally to form 3 layers. Whip cream until stiff, then add the butterscotch sauce *slowly*. Ice each layer with the whipped cream and sprinkle with the Heath Bar crumbs. Spread the remaining cream on the sides and sprinkle with the remaining crumbs. Refrigerate for 6 hours.

JOHN CHADS
HOUSE:
Cocktails and Hors d'Oeuvres

High on a hill, the John Chads House overlooks the
Brandywine River in Chadds Ford, Pennsylvania

$\mathbf{J}$OHN CHADS was the eldest son of Francis Chads (originally Chadsey), who had emigrated with his wife from Wiltshire, England, in early 1689. The elder Chads was typical of early Colonial men in that he, too, was an adventurous young man who searched for new lands. In his passage through Pennsylvania, he was captivated by the beauty of the area which is known today as Chadds Ford.

In the springtime in rainy weather, the Brandywine River was so swollen that it was almost impossible to cross. Chads was asked to deal with this problem of nature when he was solicited to establish a ferry to cross the Brandywine. Since the building of this ferry—also known as a "Hatt" or "schowe"—was a public work, the county loaned him thirty pounds to meet his expenses.

Having become permanently attached to this area, in September of 1736 Chads petitioned and received from the court a license to "keep a public Inn or road from Philadelphia to Nottingham, in Birmingham." As travel increased, many places of rest were needed to accommodate the travelers. The Chads house was built of stone. Thick stone walls were used to insulate these old-fashioned taverns. They were cool in summer, warm and pleasant from the glow of their huge fireplaces in winter. The floors were usually sanded.

Since the people led a rugged and laborious life, they had less opportunity for esthetic culture than we do today. Their pleasures consisted largely in the gratification of their appetites. The drinking of beer and distilled liquors was common among all classes.

At taverns in Colonial days, the landlord filled small glasses known as "jiggers," and if the imbiber was not satisfied, he had to pay for his second drink.

A drink popular in early American taverns was the Flip. Following, on the left, is The original recipe for the drink and on the right, a modern version of the same.

American Flip

American flip was made in a great pewter mug or earthen pitcher filled two-thirds full of strong beer; sweetened with sugar, molasses or dried pumpkin, according to individual tastes or capabilities, and flavored with "a dash"—about a gill—of New England Rum. Into this mixture was thrust and stirred a red-hot loggerhead, made of iron and shaped like a poker, and the seething iron made the liquor foam and bubble and mantle high and gave it the burnt, bitter taste so dearly loved.

For a special fancy in flip, the landlord mixed together a pint of cream, four eggs, and four pounds of sugar, and kept this on hand. When a mug of flip was called for, he filled a great mug two-thirds full of bitter beer, added four great spoonfuls of his creamy compound and a gill of rum, and thrust in the loggerhead. If a fresh egg were beaten into the mixture the froth poured over the top of the mug, and the drink was called "bellous-top."

Ale Flip

2 quarts beer
1 lemon
½ oz. cinnamon
4 tsp. brown sugar
1 glass Ale
12 eggs

Be sure to have on hand two large pitchers. Break the eggs and separate the whites. Remove the peel from the lemon and cut in thin strips. Put the beer and ale in a large saucepan, add lemon peel, cinnamon and sugar, and bring to a boil. Beat the egg whites in a large bowl. Remove the saucepan from the fire and pour its contents onto the beaten-up egg whites. Without stirring the mixture, empty it into one of the pitchers. Pour it smartly back and forth from pitcher to pitcher, until the froth is deep. Serve in glass mugs.

Courtesy of C. Schmidt & Sons, Inc.

The entrance hall of Chads House

A cooking pot
hangs in the
kitchen fireplace

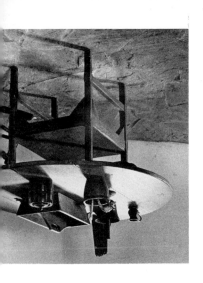

Come . . . *Cinq à Sept*

(serves 10–12)

★ BARBECUED HOT DOGS

★ COMPANY CHEESE BALL

★ CURRY DIP

★ MUSHROOMS À LA KIT

★ HOT SWISS SANDWICH PUFFS

★ HOT CRAB SPREAD

Barbecued Hot Dogs

2½ lb. hot dogs, cut into bite-size pieces
two 12-oz. jars red currant jelly
6-oz. jar Dijon mustard

Melt jelly and add mustard. Heat thoroughly and add hot dogs. Simmer for 15 minutes. Serve in chafing dish with toothpicks. May be made ahead and reheated.

Company Cheese Ball

8 oz. package cream cheese
2 cups Wispride cheese
3 oz. Roquefort cheese, crumbled
2½ tbsp. worcestershire sauce
garlic salt to taste
½ to ¾ cup sour cream
chopped nuts

A day before serving, mix together all ingredients except nuts. Chill overnight. When ready to use, form into a ball and roll in chopped nuts.

Curry Dip

3 cups mayonnaise
3 tsp. curry
2 tbsp. grated onion
1 tsp. dry mustard
1 tsp. salt
1 tsp. pepper
few drops Tabasco

Mix all ingredients together with electric beater. Chill at least 2 hours. Serve with raw vegetables: carrots, cauliflower, broccoli, radishes, etc.

Mushrooms à la Kit

¾ lb. fresh medium mushrooms
3-oz. package cream cheese
3–4 tbsp. minced clams, well drained
minced onion to taste
1 tbsp. mayonnaise
1 tsp. horseradish
Parmesan cheese

Mix together all ingredients, except mushrooms and Parmesan cheese. Remove stems from mushrooms. Stuff with mixture. Sprinkle with Parmesan. Bake 15–20 minutes at 350° F.

Hot Swiss Sandwich Puffs

worcestershire sauce
1 cup mayonnaise
½ cup chopped onion
2 tbsp. parsley
Swiss cheese
crackers

Combine mayonnaise, worcestershire sauce to taste, onion, and parsley. Spread on crackers and top with a piece of Swiss cheese. Broil 2–3 minutes.

Hot Crab Spread

3 8-oz. packages cream cheese
3 small packages frozen crabmeat
½ cup minced onion
grated cheddar cheese
party rye rounds

Soften cream cheese. Thaw and drain crabmeat. Mix together cream cheese, crabmeat, and onion. Put in small casserole. Sprinkle with grated cheese. Bake at 350° F for 15 minutes. Serve with rye bread rounds.

Spring Bash for Fifty

★ BRUNSWICK PUNCH

ASSORTED CHEESES AND

FRESH SOUR DOUGH BREAD

★ COCKTAIL MEATBALLS

★ HOT SPINACH HORS D'OEUVRES

★ FRUIT FONDUE

★ TAPENADE

★ STUFFED MUSHROOMS

★ HOT CHEESE HORS D'OEUVRES

★ GALA PECAN SPREAD

Brunswick Punch

3 bottles sauterne
1 bottle sherry
1 bottle brandy
⅓ bottle rum, to taste
3 bottles sparkling water, chilled

On the day before serving, combine first four ingredients. Chill. Add sparkling water just before serving, after ice is in. *Do not stir.*

Cocktail Meatballs

3 lb. meat loaf mix
1 scant cup bread crumbs
1 cup milk
2 tbsp. salt
1 tsp. pepper
¼ tsp. garlic powder
¼ tsp. garlic salt
1 tbsp. dry spaghetti mix
¼ cup romano cheese
2 eggs, well beaten
1 large jar spaghetti sauce

Mix together all but the spaghetti sauce. Simmer in hot oil. Cook 20 minutes in spaghetti sauce.

Hot Spinach Hors d'Oeuvres

four 10-oz. packages chopped frozen spinach
4 cups Pepperidge Farm herb stuffing
2 large onions, diced
8 eggs
1 cup Parmesan cheese
1½ cups butter, melted
1 tbsp. thyme
2 garlic cloves, minced
salt and pepper

Cook spinach and drain. Squeeze out liquid when draining spinach. Mix all ingredients together well. Chill 2 hours or more. Roll into balls 1″ in diameter. Freeze or refrigerate until ready to use. Cook about 30 minutes at 300° F until golden brown.

Fruit Fondue

10-oz. package frozen strawberries, peaches, or raspberries (or
    1½ cups canned fruit)
1 tsp. lime juice
2 tbsp. Grand Marnier
¼ cup light cream, or half and half
1 tsp. cornstarch

pound cake cubes
marshmallows
cubes of fresh fruit

Thaw fruit, do not drain. Place all ingredients, except the final 3 items, in blender. Run at high speed until smooth. Pour into fondue pot and heat until slightly thickened, stirring occasionally. Keep heat on low, and serve with assorted "dippers."

Tapenade

2 cups mayonnaise
6-oz. can tuna fish
1½ anchovy fillets
3 tbsp. chopped pitted black olives
1 scallion
2 garlic cloves
¼ cup chopped celery
¼ cup cream of potato soup
½ tsp. worcestershire sauce
dash of Tabasco

Place all ingredients into blender. Blend until well mixed and smooth. Serve with fresh vegetables such as: peppers, raw mushrooms, cauliflower, broccoli, celery, carrots, and radishes.

Stuffed Mushrooms

4–6 lb. medium-size fresh mushrooms (about 20 to the lb.)
4 lb. bulk sausage (mild or hot)

Wash mushrooms under running water. Do not peel. Remove stems. Reserve stems for other uses. Fill mushroom caps with sausage. Bake for 20–30 minutes at 350° F. Serve with toothpicks. Can be prepared a day ahead and cooked before serving.

Hot Cheese Hors d'Oeuvres

1 lb. sharp cheddar cheese
½ lb. uncooked bacon
20 slices white bread, slightly toasted
medium onion, quartered

Mix cheese, onion and bacon together in meat grinder. Remove crust from toast. Spread with mixture. Bake at 450° F for 10 minutes or until it bubbles. Cut into quarters.

Gala Pecan Spread

two 8-oz. packages cream cheese
two 2½-oz. jars dried beef, or equivalent fresh dried beef
4 tbsp. dehydrated onion flakes
¼ tsp. garlic powder
1 cup sour cream
freshly ground pepper
1 cup coarsely chopped pecans
4 tbsp. butter
½ tsp. salt

Combine cheese and sour cream until smooth and well blended. Add dried beef, onion flakes, and seasonings. Spoon into 2-qt. soufflé dish. Set aside. Melt butter in pan, add pecans and bake at 300° F for 20 minutes. Sprinkle salt over nuts and cool. Cover cheese mixture with nuts and bake at 350° F for 30 minutes. Serve with melba toast.

> ## *Before the Dinner Dance*
> (serves 10)
> ★ MINIATURE QUICHES
> ★ CHICKEN LIVER–WATER CHESTNUT BROIL
> ★ HOT CRAB AND CHEESE DIP
> MARINATED CHERRY TOMATOES

Miniature Quiches

Pastry shells
>½ cup butter
>3-oz. package cream cheese
>1 cup unsifted flour

Filling
>1 large egg, slightly beaten
>½ cup milk
>¼ tsp. salt
>1 cup grated Swiss cheese

Cream butter and cream cheese. Work in flour. Chill if soft. Roll into 24 balls and press each into small muffin pan cups.

Combine egg, milk, and salt. Fill the pastry shells with the grated cheese. Dribble the egg mixture over the cheese. Bake in a 350° F oven for 30 minutes. Serve warm. Makes 24.

Chicken Liver–Water Chestnut Broil

Marinade

¾ cup soya sauce
⅛ tsp. ground ginger
⅛ cup sherry
1 clove garlic, crushed
dash of pepper

½ lb. chicken livers, halved
½ lb. water chestnuts, halved
bacon slices, halved
brown sugar

Combine marinade ingredients and marinate chicken livers for 6 hours. Dry the livers and the water chestnuts. Wrap bacon around chicken liver and water chestnut and spear with wooden toothpicks. Dust with brown sugar and broil.

Hot Crab and Cheese Dip

8-oz. package cream cheese
2 tbsp. milk
6-oz. can crabmeat
pinch of salt
1 tsp. grated onion
1 tbsp. horseradish
1 tbsp. worcestershire
Tabasco, to taste
slivered almonds
1 tsp. lemon juice

Cream cheese with milk—add crabmeat, salt, horseradish, worcestershire sauce, lemon juice, onion, and Tabasco. Mix well. Pour into buttered casserole and sprinkle with almonds. Bake ½ hour at 375° F. Serve hot with favorite crackers.

. . . *Around the Pool*

(serves 10–12)

ASSORTED FRUITS IN WATERMELON BOAT

★ EGGPLANT CAVIAR

★ PÂTÉ

★ STEAK TARTARE

★ PEPPER CLAM SHELLS

★ DILL DIP WITH FRESH VEGETABLES

Eggplant Caviar

1 eggplant
1 onion, diced and sautéed in olive oil
1 green pepper (if you want a hot Mexican dish, use ½ can
    ortega mild diced chiles instead of 1 green pepper)
1 clove garlic, sautéed
2 tomatoes, peeled and chopped
2 tbsp. white wine
salt and pepper, to taste

Boil whole eggplant for about 45 minutes, or until tender. Cool, peel, and chop. Sauté onion, garlic, and pepper, then add to eggplant. Add the tomatoes, wine, and seasonings. Cook over low heat until thick. Serve hot or cold on party rounds of pumpernickel.

Pâté

3 oz. liverwurst, chicken livers, or any pâté
3 oz. cream cheese
1 tbsp. whiskey
1 can consommé, undiluted
1 tbsp. gelatin
2 tbsp. cold water
1 tbsp. sherry

Mix first 3 ingredients together. Set aside. Heat consommé, soften gelatin in water and add to consommé. Add sherry. Grease a mold. Put in ½ of soup mixture. Chill enough so layer of pâté will not sink. Add pâté and refrigerate about 5 minutes. Add remaining soup. Refrigerate until firm.

Steak Tartare

1 lb. ground sirloin
1 medium onion, grated
1 clove garlic, minced
1 raw egg
1 tbsp. salad oil
1 tsp. vinegar
mustard powder
Accent
salt and pepper to taste

Mix all ingredients together and chill. Serve on small rye bread rounds.

Pepper Clam Shells

1 cup onion, chopped
1 cup celery, chopped
½ cup green pepper, chopped
½ cup butter
4 tbsp. flour
2 tbsp. grated Parmesan cheese
dash worcestershire sauce
dash Tabasco sauce
½ tsp. salt and pepper
two 8-oz. cans minced clams, with juice
30 Ritz crackers

Sauté onion, celery, and pepper in ½ cup butter. Add flour, cheese, worcestershire sauce, Tabasco sauce, salt, and pepper. Mix all in a pan and add minced clams with juice. Crush Ritz crackers and add half to the clam mixture. Fill clam shells. Add a little melted butter to the remaining crackers and sprinke on clams. Bake at 350° F for 15 minutes.

Dill Dip

1 cup sour cream
1 cup mayonnaise
1 tbsp. dried minced onion
1 tbsp. parsley
1 tbsp. tiny dill leaves
1 tbsp. beau monde (Spice Island season salt)

Mix ingredients together and chill. Serve with assorted fresh vegetables.

Trim the Tree Party

(serves 24)

★ TREE TRIM PUNCH

★ YULE CHEESE LOG

★ WEVER MANSION BANDANA BENEDICTINE

★ YUMMY NUTS

★ SEAFOOD SPREAD

★ BOURBON DATES

★ MRS. FELLER'S FRUITCAKE

★ BELGIAN WAFFLE COOKIES

Tree Trim Punch

23 oz. canned pineapple juice
8 oz. frozen lemon juice (do not reconstitute)
8 oz. frozen orange juice (reconstitute)
½ gal. blended whiskey
20 oz. sugar syrup (can use light corn syrup)
two and a half 28-oz. bottles club soda

Make an ice ring with cherries and orange slices frozen in it. Combine and chill ingredients (minus club soda) ahead, stirring to mix syrup. Add ice ring and club soda.

Yule Cheese Log

8-oz. package cream cheese
4-oz package dried beef, shredded well
two 3-oz. packages chive cream cheese
1 tsp. worcestershire
1 tbsp. fresh chives, chopped

Let cheeses soften at room temperature. Combine cheeses, dried beef, and worcestershire in mixer. Form into loaf and chill. Top with chopped chives and serve with Ritz crackers.

Wever Mansion Bandana Benedictine

1 cucumber, peeled
1 onion, peeled
8-oz. package Philadelphia cream cheese, softened
mayonnaise to taste
salt to taste
2 drops Tabasco or Red Hot sauce
2 drops green food coloring
fresh watercress (optional)

Blend the cucumber and the onion coarsely in blender (or grind in food grinder or chop by hand finely) and place in a cheesecloth "bandana"—a cheesecloth square with all four corners tied together. Press out all possible juice. (You can let the bandana hang overnight tied to the spigot of the kitchen sink instead of pressing it.)

Mash the cream cheese with a fork in a bowl. Add the cucumber–onion mixture. Add salt and Tabasco to taste. Add sufficient mayonnaise to make it spreadable and add 2 drops of green food coloring. (Be careful not to overdo this; you want a cool, pale green color.) Garnish with fresh watercress, if desired. Serve at room temperature, but refrigerate for storage in covered container for a maximum of 3 days. Variation: add 1 pt. sour cream and serve as a dip.

Historical Note

Wever Mansion Bandana Benedictine is the modern version of a recipe which has been served in the James Roberts family for over 125 years. It was first served in the hospitable home of General John R. Wever and his wife, née Jean Douglas, maternal great grandparents of Roberts. Wever Mansion is near Trenton, Edgefield County, South Carolina. It was built in 1800 across from a busy log trading post and inn, called Pine Tavern, at the convergence of principal trails of the Cherokee Nations. In the 1760s, these developed into major trade routes from the uplands down to "Charles Town," now Charleston. About 300 Colonial traders produced over $250,000 worth of pelts for the Crown each year during that decade. General Wever's main business was the growing of cotton.

Wever Mansion was the first structure of sawn timber in the county and it accounts for the name of the local village, Pine House. It has sixteen rooms, eight columns supporting the front veranda, and eight columns in the rear. Nearby is the original one-story guest house. The original Wever Mansion was gutted by fire on Christmas Eve 1868, but was rebuilt by forty-six adult workers within 2 years. Their remarkable workmanship is evident in the interior woodcarvings and the exterior columns. Restoration was completed with the addition of a boxwood border to the front walkway and with ruby glass panels etched in Venice for the front and rear doors, which were transported from the outside world to Wever Mansion on the Southern Railway, which had just reached Trenton in 1870.

A contemporary letter records that "gaiety, gaming and lavishness prevailed in opulence heretofore unseen" at Wever Mansion in the 1850s. It is also reported that this appetizer recipe was served in the spread version at a party,

Yummy Nuts

¼ cup butter
½ tsp. Tabasco sauce
1 tsp. worcestershire sauce
¾ tbsp. garlic salt
2 cups shelled pecan halves
¼ tsp. nutmeg

Melt butter. Add spices. Add nuts and spoon ingredients over nuts. Toast in pan in oven at 375° F for 12 minutes, until brown. Shake them often!!! Drain on brown paper.

Seafood Spread

1 tbsp. butter
2 stalks celery, finely chopped
½ green pepper, finely chopped
1 tbsp. worcestershire sauce
¾ cup mayonnaise
1 tbsp. lemon juice
6 saltines, crushed
6½-oz. can of shrimp, or ¾ cup cooked fresh shrimp
7-oz. can crab, or ¾ cup fresh crab
scant ¼ tsp. salt
⅛ tsp. pepper
¼ cup Parmesan cheese, grated

Sauté celery, green pepper, and worcestershire sauce in butter until celery and green peppers are tender. Add mayonnaise. Pour lemon

from which also survives an elegantly printed invitation, indicating that a young lady "is respectfully invited to attend a Ball, to be given at the home of General and Mrs. John R. Wever, on Wednesday evening, 15th instant, at 6 o'clock p.m., January 1, 1851."

Wever Mansion was sold to Benjamin Bettis and his wife, née Elizabeth Miller, who owned Pine Tavern, and they changed the name of the estate to Pine House. Bettis' descendants, named Bouknight, sold the mansion to J. Marshall Vann, Sr., in 1934. His widow was still living in the mansion in the 1950s; at that time, her son Marshall, Jr., and his wife, née Mary Porter Phinizy, lived in the original guest house. In 1950, Marshall Vann, Jr., won the South Carolina Five-Acre Contest with an official yield of 4,295 pounds of lint cotton. He also raised peaches, pecans, and asparagus on the land.

Today the house may be found at the junction of U.S. Highway 25 and South Carolina State Highway 19, just west of Trenton in Edgefield County. Pine Tavern no longer exists.

juice over crabmeat and shrimp. Add to first mixture. Put into greased casserole and top with crushed saltines and cheese. Dot with butter and bake in preheated 350° F oven for 20–30 minutes, until brown.

Bourbon Dates

Pit dates, soak in bourbon overnight. Put pecans in center and roll in granulated sugar. Store in tin and keep several weeks.

Mrs. Feller's Fruitcake

    2 lb. white raisins
    2 cups candied cherries
    2 cups candied pineapple
    2 cups citron
    ½ cup lemon peel
    1 cup blanched, sliced almonds
    3 cups whole pecans
    1 jar apricot preserves
    1 cup angel flake coconut
    1½ cups pineapple juice
    2 tbsp. vanilla
    3½ cups flour
    ½ lb. butter
    1 lb. light brown sugar
    10 eggs
    1 tsp. salt
    1 tsp. nutmeg
    1 tsp. allspice
    ½ cup brandy
    ½ cup rum
    ½ cup sherry

Mix fruits, nuts, preserves, and coconut. Cover with pineapple juice and let stand overnight. Next day, drain fruit and mix with ½ cup of the flour, then set aside. Cream butter and sugar together. Add eggs one at a time. Sift together 3 cups of flour, salt, nutmeg, and allspice. Gradually add to butter and egg mixture. Fold in fruit mixture. Place in 2 tube pans lined with waxed paper. Bake at 250° F for 3 hours (start watching after 2 hours). Remove and cool thoroughly. Pour liquor on cakes and allow to stand overnight.

Belgian Waffle Cookies

1¼ lb. butter
8 eggs, separated
2 cups white sugar
2 cups brown sugar (packed firmly)
6 cups flour
1 tsp. salt
1 tsp. cinnamon
1 tsp. almond extract
1 tbsp. vanilla

Cream butter and sugars; add egg yolks, cinnamon, salt, and flavorings. Beat for 2 minutes with electric beater. Add 3 cups flour, then fold in stiffly beaten egg whites. Add remaining 3 cups of flour. Bake on a French-Belgian waffle iron over medium heat for about 2 minutes on each side.

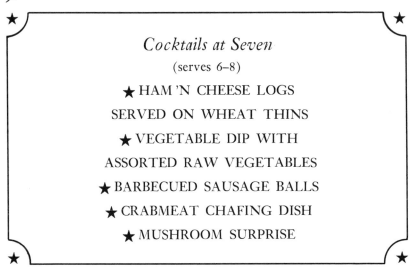

Cocktails at Seven

(serves 6–8)

★ HAM 'N CHEESE LOGS

SERVED ON WHEAT THINS

★ VEGETABLE DIP WITH

ASSORTED RAW VEGETABLES

★ BARBECUED SAUSAGE BALLS

★ CRABMEAT CHAFING DISH

★ MUSHROOM SURPRISE

Ham 'n Cheese Logs

4 oz. sharp cheese, shredded (1 cup)
8-oz. package of softened cream cheese
½ cup finely chopped ripe olives
4½-oz. can deviled ham
½ cup finely chopped pecans

Have cheeses at room temperature. In a small bowl, beat together both cheeses until well blended. Beat in ham, then stir in olives. Shape into 2 rolls or balls. Chill, then roll in the chopped pecans.

Vegetable Dip

¼ lb. Roquefort cheese
1 tbsp. anchovy paste
⅛ tsp. garlic powder
¼ cup chopped scallions
¼ cup parsley flakes
1½ tsp. lemon juice
1 cup mayonnaise
½ cup sour cream

Mix ingredients together and chill for at least 2 hours before serving.

Barbecued Sausage Balls

1 lb. pork sausage
1 slightly beaten egg
⅓ cup dry bread crumbs
½ tsp. sage
½ cup catsup
2 tbsp. brown sugar
1 tbsp. vinegar
1 tbsp. soy sauce

Mix sausage, egg, bread crumbs, and sage. Shape into about 2 dozen 1″ balls. Brown in ungreased skillet slowly for about 15 minutes. Pour off excess fat. Combine remaining ingredients. Pour over meat. Cover and simmer 30 minutes, stirring occasionally to coat balls.

Crabmeat Chafing Dish

¼ lb. Old English cheese
¼ lb. butter
1 lb. crabmeat (or 2 small cans crabmeat)

Melt butter and cheese in top of double boiler, then add crab. Cook 5 minutes. Serve from chafing dish, using spoon to dip spread onto Triscuits.

Mushroom Surprise

1 lb. fresh mushrooms
1 small onion, diced
1 clove garlic, crushed
1 cup Italian bread crumbs
¼ cup olive oil
¼ cup cheddar cheese, grated
chopped parsley
grated Parmesan cheese
1 cup burgundy

Remove stems from mushrooms. Chop and add onion, garlic, and bread crumbs. Place mushroom caps in olive oil and simmer 3 minutes. Place mixture in each cap. Sprinkle with grated cheeses and parsley. Add wine and simmer for 2 minutes. Place under broiler until brown.

CLIVEDEN:
Magnificent Dining

Cliveden in Germantown, Pennsylvania, at dusk

ON October 4, 1777, during the Battle of Germantown, the British forced General Washington to retreat from the stately countryseat, Cliveden. This outstanding Georgian home was owned by Benjamin Chew (1722–1810), one of Philadelphia's distinguished lawyers and political leaders. Chew, as typical of other prominent Philadelphians, incorporated many Palladian elements into the design of his home. The gracious way of life of this family is demonstrated by the elegance of the furnishings.

John Adams notes that he:

> Dined with Mr. Chew, Chief Justice of the Province, with all the Gentlemen from Virginia, Dr. Shippen, Mr. Tilghman and many others. We were shown into a grand Entry and Stair Case, and into an elegant and most magnificent Chamber, until Dinner. About four O'Clock We were called down to Dinner. The Furniture was all Rich.—Turttle, Whip'd Syllabubbs, floating Islands, fools—etc., and then a Desert of Fruits, Raisins, Almonds, Pears, Peaches—Wines most excellent and admirable. I drank Madeira at a great Rate and found no Inconvenience in it.

A Colonial dinner was characterized by abundance rather than by elegance. Untroubled by vitamins and calories, undaunted by food values, the diners struggled merrily and bravely through overwhelming repasts. The feast, for it was nothing less, was not served in a long series of courses, but in two which very thoroughly duplicated each other. Every dish for each course was put on the table at the same time, the hot dishes under covers.

The table stretched nearly the full length of the room and was covered by a cloth—diaper clothe for everyday, a more imposing material for festive occasions. The symmetrical arrangement of the dishes on the table was of utmost importance and usually constituted the sole adornment. Flowers were seldom used; fine pieces of silver occasionally ornamented the table. After the second course, the cloth was removed from the table; fresh glasses, decanters of wine, fruit and nuts were provided. At this point, the ladies retired. However, as a rule, dinner parties were confined almost exclusively to men and occasionally included the wife of the host.

The Cliveden dining room: fruit centerpiece features a
pineapple as the symbol of Colonial hospitality, shown on
the three-part Hepplewhite mahogany table c. 1780

This dessert plate with C for Chew is
Chinese Export Porcelain c. 1788

The fireplace in the Cliveden dining room.
The chairs are Sheraton painted fancy chairs

The Chew coin silver tea service c. 1820, containing
two teapots, sugar, creamer, slop bowl, tongs, and stand

4   For Veal Collops

Make Gravey as before get oysters Cox Combs
Mushirrooms Oxes pallits & Veal Sweet breads; thes
must be prepared to put in your Sauce by Scalding &
Cutting them in pieces — Note the pallits must be Scald
Boyling tander and then Blancht y Cox Combs fur
Scalded then Blancht with a little Salt the rest fea
enough You may leave out these w.ch you will but
before have ready some forc Meat as here after and
make some into Balls w.ch you may boil or frye and
Some put in puff paust which is Call'd pattets there
Bake. . . . .
Then take a fillit of Veal & Cut off the Udder w.ch
Stuff with some forc meat and Rost for the middle of
the Dish . . . . _____

Then Cutt out 6 or 8 Slices thicker then the rest w.ch
lard with Bacon and Sprinkle with minct parsly, time
and Limmon a parcel of each & mixt with some grated
bread and a little pepper, Salt These put by and broy
Then Cut out the rest into thin Slices hack it with the
Back of a knife Larde some and fry all with a
little fresh butter over a quick fire - - - and keep warm

ecipe for Veal Collops from Deborah Norris Logan's Cookbook,
arch, 1715 *(Courtesy of Stenton, Germantown)*

The origin of the
marble statues on
Cliveden's lawn is
unknown, but
according to a writer
of the time, they were
already weatherworn
before receiving
their scars during the
Battle of Germantown,
1777

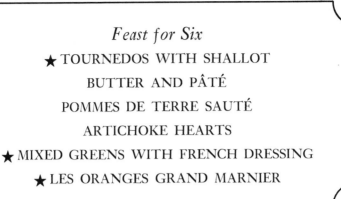

Feast for Six

★ TOURNEDOS WITH SHALLOT
BUTTER AND PÂTÉ

POMMES DE TERRE SAUTÉ

ARTICHOKE HEARTS

★ MIXED GREENS WITH FRENCH DRESSING

★ LES ORANGES GRAND MARNIER

Tournedos with Shallot Butter and Pâté

2–3 lb. filet of beef
6 slices white bread
4¾-oz. can liver pâté, chilled
2 tbsp. butter or margarine
2 cloves garlic, crushed
1 tsp. pepper
¼ cup dry white wine or red wine
2 tbsp. chopped shallots
8 tbsp. butter
1 tbsp. chopped parsley
¼ tsp. salt
⅛ tsp. white pepper
½ chopped garlic clove

With a sharp knife, cut filet crosswise into 6 steaks, each about ½″ thick. Brush all over with a mixture of 2 tbsp. melted butter or margarine and 2 cloves garlic, crushed. Sprinkle with 1 tsp. pepper. Set aside. Make shallot butter (recipe follows).

Toast 6 slices white bread. Trim to same size as steaks. Slice 1 can liver pâté into 6 round slices. (It must be well chilled first, or it won't be easy to slice.) Place steaks on rack of broiler pan. Broil 4″ from heat for 4 minutes. Turn, broil 3 or 4 minutes longer for rare. Place each steak on a toast round, then top with a slice of liver pâté and a generous spoonful of shallot butter. Serve at once.

Shallot Butter

In saucepan, combine wine and chopped shallot and garlic. Bring to a boil over high heat and boil until almost all liquid is evaporated. Remove from heat. Beat in ½ cup butter or regular margarine, a little at a time until creamy. Then beat in chopped parsley, salt, and pepper until well blended. Keep butter in warm place but do not let it melt.

Holden's French Dressing

2 cups oil
½ cup vinegar
¾ tbsp. salt
½ cup confectioners' sugar
¾ tbsp. dry mustard
¾ tbsp. paprika
juice of 1½ oranges
juice of 1½ lemons
½ tbsp. worcestershire sauce
½ clove garlic

Beat oil and vinegar together in electric mixer until thick. Mix together sugar, salt, mustard, and paprika. Add to oil and vinegar and beat. Finally, add the orange and lemon juices, worcestershire sauce, and garlic. Keeps well in quart jar in refrigerator.

Les Oranges Grand Marnier

4 fresh oranges
½ qt. orange sherbet
Grand Marnier

Section fresh oranges and freeze 20 minutes. Before serving, remove oranges from freezer. Surround scoops of sherbet with oranges and pour Grand Marnier over all.

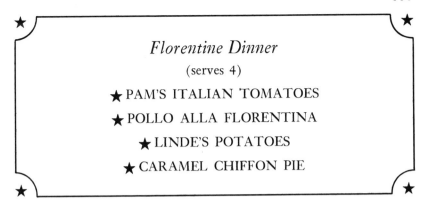

Florentine Dinner

(serves 4)

★ PAM'S ITALIAN TOMATOES

★ POLLO ALLA FLORENTINA

★ LINDE'S POTATOES

★ CARAMEL CHIFFON PIE

Pam's Italian Tomatoes

4 ripe tomatoes
2 cloves garlic
1 tbsp. olive oil
1 tsp. basil
salt
pepper

Peel tomatoes and cut into wedges. Rub salad bowl with 1 clove of the garlic and place tomatoes in it. Press the other garlic clove over the tomatoes; add the oil, basil, salt, and pepper to taste. Mix gently with a wooden spoon. Let stand in refrigerator for at least 3 hours before serving. (The longer it stands, the better.) Serve on lettuce leaves.

Pollo Alla Florentina

4 chicken breasts, boned
8 oz. butter
salt
pepper
2 bay leaves
½ cup white wine
1 lb. spinach or 2 boxes, semicooked and drained
4 tbsp. flour
1 pt. cream or milk
8 slices mozzarella cheese
dash of nutmeg
8 slices prosciutto, or other thinly sliced ham
4 oz. grated Parmesan cheese

Flatten the breasts and sauté in half the butter. Season with salt and pepper. Add bay leaves and wine; cook until the juices are clear. Remove the chicken and keep warm. Cook the spinach in the butter–wine mixture. In another pan, melt the rest of the butter, and whisk in the flour. Add the cream, and stir until thickened. Add 4 slices of the mozzarella, salt and pepper to taste, and nutmeg. Cook over moderate heat for 3–4 minutes.

Lightly butter 4 individual casseroles or 1 large casserole. Place spinach in first, then chicken, then ham (2 slices each for the individual dishes), and the remaining mozzarella (1 slice for each individual dish). Pour on the sauce, sprinkle with the Parmesan, and place under the broiler until hot and bubbly.

Linde's Potatoes

4 potatoes, peeled
½–¾ cup butter or margarine
¼ tsp. salt
¼ tsp. paprika or cayenne pepper
2 tbsp. grated Parmesan cheese
1 tbsp. Progresso seasoned bread crumbs

Slice potatoes three fourths of the way through at ¼″ intervals to make "fans." Melt butter in baking pan, roll potatoes in it to coat, and place cut-side up. Sprinkle with salt and paprika. Bake at 350° F for 45 minutes, basting every 15 minutes. Bake 20 minutes longer without basting. Blend cheese and crumbs, sprinkle on top of potatoes, and bake 10 minutes longer. Garnish with fresh parsley.

Caramel Chiffon Pie

23 light Kraft caramels
¾ cup water
½ envelope unflavored gelatin
½ tsp. vanilla
1 cup heavy cream, whipped
1 cup pecans, chopped
9″ *baked* pie shell

Melt the caramels with ½ cup of the water over low heat in double boiler, stirring until smooth. Soften the gelatin in the rest of the water, then stir into the caramel sauce. Stir in the vanilla. Chill until slightly thickened. Fold in the cream and ¾ cup of the pecans. Pour into the pie shell. Sprinkle the rest of the nuts on top and chill until firm.

Country Dinner
(serves 8)

GRILLED PORK CHOPS WITH BARBEQUE SAUCE

★ JOANNA'S BAKED PINEAPPLE

★ SCALLOPED MUSHROOMS

★ MARINATED ASPARAGUS SALAD

★ POACHED PEACHES

Joanna's Baked Pineapple

½ cup butter
1 cup sugar
4 eggs
No. 2 can crushed pineapple, well drained
5 slices white bread, cubed

Cream together butter and sugar. Add eggs and beat well. Add pineapple, stir in bread cubes. Bake in well-greased 1½-qt. casserole, uncovered at 350° F for 45 minutes to 1 hour, or until lightly browned. Serve hot or cold as a meat accompaniment.

Scalloped Mushrooms

2 lb. fresh mushrooms
1 qt. buttered, seasoned (salt & pepper) bread crumbs
½ cup cream
½ cup liquor from mushrooms (from cooking)
2–3 tbsp. butter
salt and pepper to taste

Wash mushrooms and slice. Brown in skillet with the butter, salt, and pepper. Cover and cook slowly about 20–25 minutes. Drain, saving liquor. Put layer of buttered bread crumbs in baking dish, then layer of mushrooms. Repeat. Top with bread crumbs. Mix cream and mushroom liquor and pour over all. Bake for 20 minutes in a 350° F oven.

Marinated Asparagus Salad

2 lb. asparagus
1 large red onion, sliced
1 cucumber, peeled and sliced
bibb or Boston lettuce

Wash and clean asparagus spears. Cook until just tender. Marinate asparagus, onion slices, and cucumber slices in dressing (recipe follows) for several hours or overnight. Place on lettuce leaves and pour a little dressing over all.

Dressing
1⅓ cups olive oil
⅔ cup tarragon vinegar
2 tbsp. lemon juice
2 garlic cloves, mashed
2 tsp. salt
1 tbsp. sugar
1 tsp. dill weed
1 tsp. dry mustard
¼ cup Durkee's dressing

Combine all ingredients in bottle or cruet and shake well. Pour over vegetables and let marinate for several hours or overnight; the longer they marinate, the better they taste. Yields 2 cups of dressing.

Poached Peaches

1 large can Freestone peaches, undrained
light brown sugar
sour cream
cinnamon

Heat peaches and liquid over medium heat. *Do not boil.* Use 1 peach half per serving and fill each with sugar and sour cream, and sprinkle cinnamon on top. Pour small amount of liquid on top of each peach.

Summer Barbecue

(serves 4–6)

★ MARINATED LONDON BROIL

★ ZESTY ZUCCHINI

LETTUCE WEDGE WITH ★ RUSSIAN DRESSING

HARD ROLLS AND BUTTER

★ CHOCOLATE PIE

Marinated London Broil

2½–3 lb. London broil

Marinade
    1 can beer
    ½ cup peanut or vegetable oil
    1 tsp. dry mustard
    ½ tsp. ginger
    ½ tsp. worcestershire sauce
    1 tbsp. sugar
    2 tbsp. orange or ginger marmalade
    1 tsp. garlic powder
    salt and freshly ground pepper, to taste

Mix all ingredients together and pour into *glass* oblong casserole. Place meat in mixture and spoon over top and sides. Cover and place in refrigerator for 24 hours. Turn meat at least twice for even marinating. When ready to serve, reserve some marinade for brushing on meat at cooking time. Barbecue to personal taste.

Zesty Zucchini

    1 large zucchini, unpeeled and sliced
    1 large onion, sliced
    1 large tomato, peeled and sliced
    6 slices cooked bacon
    4 slices American cheese
    8 oz. sharp cheese, grated ⎱ mixed
    ¼ cup grated Swiss cheese ⎰

Grease 2-qt. casserole. Line bottom with American cheese. Alternate layers of zucchini, onion, tomato, cheeses, ending with cheeses on top. Bake at 350° F for 1 hour. Fifteen minutes before serving, put bacon slices on top of dish.

Russian Dressing

1 cup mayonnaise
½ cup chili sauce
1 hard-boiled egg, chopped
2 tbsp. sweet relish
1 tbsp. Durkee's mustard sauce
½ tsp. prepared horseradish
1 tsp. sugar
dash of worcestershire sauce
squeeze of lemon juice
salt and freshly ground pepper, to taste
dash of dried parsley leaves

Mix above ingredients together. Chill until ready to serve. Makes approximately 2 cups.

Chocolate Pie

1 prepared graham cracker crust

or:

14 plain or honey graham crackers
½ cup butter

Filling

½ cup butter
¾ cup sugar
2 squares Hershey's unsweetened chocolate, melted
1 tbsp. vanilla
2 eggs
½ pt. whipping cream
grated chocolate

Finely crush graham crackers with rolling pin between 2 sheets of waxed paper. Mix with ½ cup melted butter. Press firmly into sides and bottom of 9″ pie plate. Refrigerate. Can be done a day ahead.

Cream butter and sugar together until smooth and fluffy. Add melted chocolate and vanilla, beating well. Next add eggs, one at a time, beating each one for 5 minutes into mixture. Pour into pie crust and chill until set. Before serving, whip cream and spread on top of pie. Garnish with grated chocolate.

Casserole Buffet

(serves 16)

★ CHICKEN SAUSAGE CASSEROLE

TOSSED SALAD WITH

★ BONNIE'S ITALIAN DRESSING

CRESCENT ROLLS

★ RUM CAKE

Chicken Sausage Casserole

4 to 6 large, whole chicken breasts
2–3 cups fresh or canned chicken broth
4 hot Italian sausages
½ cup + 2 tbsp. butter
6 tbsp. flour
1 cup heavy cream
3–4 chopped onions
2 cups chopped green pepper
2 cups chopped celery
4 cups tomato sauce
2 tsp. minced garlic
1–2 lb. ground round steak
2 bay leaves
2 cups thinly sliced mushrooms
1 lb. spaghetti
2½ cups cooked peas (2 boxes frozen)
1 lb. cheddar cheese, grated
worcestershire sauce
Tabasco sauce

Simmer chicken until tender, about 25 minutes. Should yield about
8 cups of cooked meat. Bake sausage at 450° F about 15 minutes.
Drain. Melt 6 tbsp. of butter in large pan. Add flour and blend. Add
2 cups broth and stir until thick. Add cream and tomato sauce. Season
with worcestershire sauce and Tabasco.

Cook onion, green pepper, and celery in small amount of oil until tender. Add garlic and beef and brown. Add tomato–cream sauce to beef. Salt and pepper to taste and add bay leaf. Sauté mushrooms in remaining butter and add to tomato–meat sauce.

Meanwhile, cook spaghetti until almost tender. Rinse in cold water. Arrange in layers in a large, deep ovenproof casserole: tomato–meat sauce, spaghetti, chicken, sliced sausage, peas, and cheese. Repeat layers, ending with cheese. Add more chicken broth if casserole seems too dry. Bake at 450° F about 45 minutes or until bubbly. Tomato–meat sauce may be made ahead and may be frozen.

Bonnie's Italian Dressing

1 cup oil
⅓ cup malt vinegar
⅓ cup catsup
¼ cup sugar
1 tsp. grated onion
3 tbsp. lemon juice
2 tsp. salt
1 tsp. pepper
1 tsp. paprika

Blend all ingredients together. Store in refrigerator.

Rum Cake

4 egg whites
8 egg yolks
1 cup sugar
2 cups all-purpose flour, sifted *before* measuring
2 tsp. double-acting baking powder
½ tsp. salt
2 tsp. vanilla
⅔ cup melted butter

Sauce

2 cups sugar
2 cups water
1 tbsp. grated orange rind
1 tbsp. + 1 tsp. lemon juice
½ cup rum
ice cream and chopped nuts

Preheat oven to 375° F. Grease a 3-qt. tube pan. Beat egg whites until fluffy, gradually adding ½ cup of the sugar and then beating until stiff. In a smaller bowl, beat the egg yolks with the remaining sugar. Then add all at once to the whites, stirring in lightly but well. Sift the flour, baking powder, and salt together and fold gently into egg mixture. Stir in vanilla and melted butter. Pour into prepared pan and bake at 375° F for about 30 minutes, or until top feels springy when touched and toothpick inserted in cake comes out clean. While cake is baking, make sauce.

Sauce

Dissolve the sugar in the water in a saucepan, then add the grated orange rind, and bring to a boil for 10 minutes. Cool a bit at room temperature while cake is baking, then add lemon juice and rum.

When cake is done, turn out onto rack. Remove waxed paper and put immediately onto serving plate. Make holes all over the top of cake through to bottom, with a skewer. Spoon on all the warm sauce with a big spoon. Make more holes if necessary. Continue basting with any sauce that ends up on bottom of plate. When cake has absorbed nearly all sauce, refrigerate, covered. To serve, fill center with ice cream sprinkled with nuts.

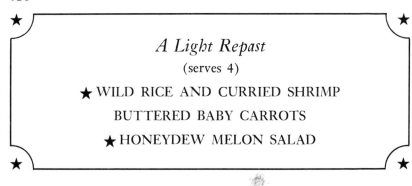

Wild Rice and Curried Shrimp

wild rice—enough for 6–8 servings
2 lb. raw shrimp, peeled and deveined
¼ cup butter
2 tbsp. flour
⅛ tsp. nutmeg
⅛ tsp. paprika
1½ pt. heavy cream
1 tbsp. curry powder

Cook rice according to package directions. Add salt and a pat of butter. Cook shrimp for 2 or 3 minutes in butter and sprinkle flour into it. Add nutmeg, salt, paprika. Stir. Add cream and curry to shrimp. Stir very rapidly. Serve from chafing dish over rice.

Condiments: chutney, chopped hard-boiled eggs, chopped peanuts, grated onion, toasted coconut.

Honeydew Melon Salad

Using small honeydew melons, peel them, then slice across to make rings. On a lettuce leaf, place a ring. Fill it with a ball made of cream cheese rolled in broken nuts and white seedless grapes. Cover with French dressing mixed with red currant jelly to taste.

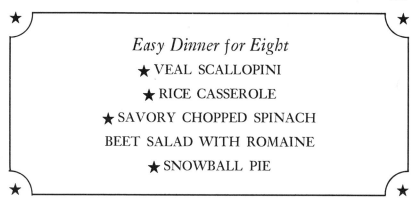

Easy Dinner for Eight

★ VEAL SCALLOPINI

★ RICE CASSEROLE

★ SAVORY CHOPPED SPINACH

BEET SALAD WITH ROMAINE

★ SNOWBALL PIE

Veal Scallopini

1 to 1½ lb. veal tenders
4 tbsp. oil
2 tbsp. butter
½ cup flour
salt
pepper
1 cup beef bouillon
1 tsp. rosemary
½ tsp. Gravy Master
1½ tbsp. lemon juice
parsley
1 cup white wine

Pound veal tenders. Dredge in flour, salt, and pepper mixture. Sauté in 2 tbsp. oil and 1 tbsp. butter. Mix bouillon with rosemary and Gravy Master. When meat is brown, add bouillon mixture. Add lemon to taste, fresh parsley, and wine. Simmer 40–50 minutes, covered. Remove veal and add additional wine for sauce if needed. Strain and pour over meat. Garnish with fresh parsley.

Rice Casserole

1 cup rice, raw
½ cup butter
1 can onion soup
1–2 cloves garlic, crushed
1 can chicken consommé
4 tbsp. Parmesan cheese

Melt butter in skillet. Brown rice about 10 minutes. Add onion soup, garlic, consommé and Parmesan cheese. Add salt and pepper to taste. Pour into casserole, cover, and bake at 325° F for 1 hour.

Savory Chopped Spinach

2 packages frozen chopped spinach, cooked and thoroughly drained
6 oz. cream cheese
1 cup sour cream
6 strips bacon; cooked and crumbled
½ cup chopped green onions
1½ tbsp. horseradish
dash salt
dash pepper

Blend cream cheese and spinach. Add rest of ingredients and mix thoroughly. Spoon into 1½-qt. casserole. Bake at 350° F for 30 minutes.

Snowball Pie

6 oz. Nestlé's semisweet chocolate bits
¼ cup butter
¼ cup Coffee Rich or milk
4 oz. sweet flaked coconut
1 qt. French vanilla ice cream
sprinkling of peppermint or shaved chocolate mint

Combine chocolate and butter and melt over top of double boiler. Add liquid and stir until blended. Remove from heat and add coconut. Allow to cool slightly (but not to harden) before lining sides and bottom of 9″ pie plate. Chill until firm.

Fill shell with ice cream and freeze. Place in refrigerator about 10 minutes before serving for easier slicing. Garnish with chocolate mint curls or crushed peppermint candy.

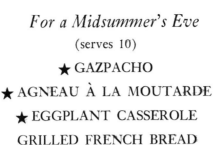

For a Midsummer's Eve

(serves 10)

★ GAZPACHO

★ AGNEAU À LA MOUTARDE

★ EGGPLANT CASSEROLE

GRILLED FRENCH BREAD

★ CHOCOLATE RUM TORTE

Gazpacho

2 cups cucumber, peeled
4 tomatoes, peeled
2 cups green pepper
6 young scallions
2–3 cloves garlic, crushed
½ tsp. salt
2½ tbsp. lemon juice
Tabasco, to taste
4 cups tomato juice, chilled
2½ cups beef consommé, chilled

Coarsely chop the cucumber, tomato, green pepper, and scallions. Add remaining ingredients and mix well. Best made a day ahead.

Agneau à la Moutarde

1 leg of lamb, boned and butterflied in one piece
8-oz. jar of Dijon mustard
½ cup olive oil with 2–3 cloves of garlic in it for 24 hours
1 tsp. crushed rosemary
1 tsp. thyme
1 tsp. bay leaves, crushed
pepper

Mix all marinade ingredients together. Slash lamb in several places and spread the marinade generously on all sides. Cover and marinate for several hours or overnight.

Broil on a charcoal grill or oven broil until the marinade is brown and the meat is pink inside. Do not overcook. Baste with marinade while cooking.

Eggplant Casserole

1 large eggplant
3 tbsp. butter, melted
3 tbsp. flour
16-oz. can tomatoes
½ cup chopped green pepper
½ cup chopped onion
1 tsp. salt
1 tbsp. brown sugar
½ bay leaf
bread crumbs
shredded cheese

Peel and dice eggplant, then cook for 10 minutes. Meanwhile, mix butter and flour in pan. Add tomatoes, pepper, and onion. Add salt, brown sugar, bay leaf; cook 5 minutes.

Place eggplant in casserole, and pour tomato mixture over it. Top with bread crumbs and cheese. Dot with butter. Bake at 350° F for 30 minutes.

May be frozen, except for bread crumbs.

Chocolate Rum Torte

1 large angel food cake
½ cup rum
four 6-oz. packages chocolate chips
6 eggs
2 tsp. vanilla
2 tbsp. sugar
1½ to 2 pt. heavy cream
¼ cup toasted, sliced almonds

Tear cake into small pieces and toss with rum. Melt chocolate in a double boiler. Turn chocolate into bowl and add eggs, one at a time, using medium speed of electric mixer. Beat in vanilla and salt. In separate bowl, beat 1 pt. cream until frothy. Add sugar, then whip to soft peaks. Fold chocolate mixture into cream. Layer chocolate mixture and cake into a well-greased 10″ tube pan. Refrigerate until firm.

Turn onto serving platter and frost with remaining cream, whipped. Garnish with almonds. Freeze at least 30 minutes (longer, if desired) covered with plastic wrap.

```
★                                                          ★
  ┌─────────────────────────────────────────────────┐
            Buffet for Twenty-Four
        ★ CHICKEN CURRY WITH CONDIMENTS
                      RICE
     FRUIT SALAD WITH ★ HONEY DRESSING
    CHOCOLATE CUPS WITH PEPPERMINT ICE CREAM
              ★ GINGERKRINKLES
  └─────────────────────────────────────────────────┘
★                                                          ★
```

Chicken Curry

16 whole chicken breasts
3 qt. Coffee Rich
2 qt. chicken stock
2 ½ cups flour
1 ¼ lb. butter
½ cup curry powder
salt, pepper, Accent to taste

Boil chicken breasts until fork tender. Drain off liquid and reduce 2 qt. of rich broth. Strain and set aside.

Sauce

Melt butter in top of double boiler, add flour and cook, stirring constantly, over low heat. Allow to thicken slightly. Slowly add 1 qt. of liquid at a time, until all liquid—including Coffee Rich and the chicken stock—has been used. Continue cooking in double boiler over water until mixture is thick and creamy. May simmer on stove for several hours. About 2 hours before serving, add cooked chicken, salt, pepper, and Accent to sauce.

Serve with the following condiments:

sweet coconut	crushed potato chips
guava jelly	chow chow (mustard pickle)
currant jelly	chutney
raisins	chopped black olives
sliced bananas	chopped peanuts

Honey Dressing

½ cup sugar
1 tsp. salt
1 tsp. mustard
1 tsp. celery salt or seed
1 tsp. paprika
1 tsp. onion juice
1 cup oil
½ cup vinegar
2 tbsp. honey

Mix 5 dry ingredients with the onion juice. Add oil and vinegar alternately, adding the oil slowly at first. Mix in the honey. Makes about 2 cups of dressing.

Gingerkrinkles

¼ cup sugar
⅔ cup oil
1 cup sugar
1 egg
4 tbsp. molasses
2 cups flour
2 tsp. soda
¼ tsp. salt
1 tsp. cinnamon
1 tsp. ginger

Preheat oven to 350° F. Mix oil and 1 cup sugar, add egg, and beat well. Stir in molasses. Sift in dry ingredients. Drop batter by teaspoonfuls into ¼ cup sugar and form balls coated with sugar. Place on cookie sheet 3″ apart. Bake 8–10 minutes at 350° F. Yields 3 dozen.

★ *Creole Dinner*

(serves 6–8)

★ STUFFED FLOUNDER

★ EGGPLANT CREOLE

TOSSED SALAD

★ POTS DE CRÈME

Stuffed Flounder

5 lb. flounder fillets
1 lb. crabmeat
½ cup chopped scallions
½ cup butter
two 3-oz. cans chopped mushrooms, drained (reserve liquid)
1 cup crumbled saltines
1 tsp. salt
parsley
6 tbsp. flour
½ tsp. salt
⅔ cup dry white wine
2 cups (8 oz.) shredded Swiss cheese
1 tsp. paprika
milk

Sauté onions in butter. Add mushrooms, crab, crackers, salt, pepper, and parsley. Stir and spread over fillets. Roll up and place in baking dish.

To make sauce, melt butter, blend in flour and salt. Add milk to reserved mushroom liquid to make 2⅔ cups, and add to sauce. Blend in wine. Pour over fish. Bake at 400° F for 25 minutes. Put shredded cheese over all for an additional 5 minutes.

Eggplant Creole

1 medium eggplant
3 large tomatoes, or 2 cups chopped canned tomatoes
1 small green pepper
1 small onion
3 tbsp. butter
3 tbsp. flour
1 tsp. salt
1 tbsp. brown sugar
½ bay leaf
2 cloves
grated cheese
bread crumbs

Peel, cut, and dice eggplant. Cook for 10 minutes in boiling water. Drain and place in baking dish. Melt butter in skillet and add flour. Peel, slice, and chop tomatoes, pepper, and onion. Add to butter mixture with salt, brown sugar, bay leaf, and cloves. Cook for 5 minutes. Pour over eggplant. Cover top with bread crumbs. Dot with butter and sprinkle with grated cheese. Bake at 350° F for 30 minutes or until bubbly.

Pots de Crème

1 cup chocolate bits, or mint chocolate bits
¾ cup scalded milk
1 tbsp. sugar
1 egg
dash vanilla
dash salt

Put in blender. Chill and serve. Makes 6 servings.

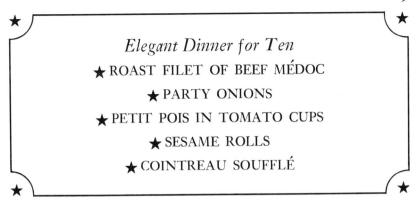

★ROAST FILET OF BEEF MÉDOC

Roast Filet of Beef Médoc

6 lb. filet mignon
½ cup tomato puree
2 cups Médoc wine
6 bouillon cubes
8 cups water
½ cup minced onions
½ cup minced carrots
½ cup minced celery
6 tbsp. butter
6 tbsp. flour
1 cup finely chopped, sautéed mushrooms
1 tbsp. lemon juice
1 tbsp. chopped parsley
sautéed mushroom caps (at least 20)
parsley

Combine the tomato puree, wine, bouillon cubes, and water. Reduce over medium heat (to reduce liquid to 5 cups should take about 2½ hours.) Cook celery, carrots, and onions in butter over low heat about 20 minutes or until tender. Put vegetables through a strainer (reserving butter) and add to the tomato–wine mixture.

Simmer liquid mixture another 15 minutes over low heat. Put through a strainer and discard vegetables.

To the reserved butter, add another 3 tbsp. melted butter or enough to equal 6 tbsp. Stirring with a wire wisk, add 1 tbsp. of flour at a time. Stir constantly to avoid lumps and cook thoroughly. Slowly add liquid to the roux (flour and butter mixture), stirring to avoid lumps. Cook until thick enough to coat spoon. Add sautéed mushrooms (chopped), lemon juice, and chopped parsley. To thin the sauce, add more wine.

To cook roast: have butcher remove fat from meat. Rub salt, pepper, and one clove crushed garlic over top of filet. Put on rack in shallow pan and bake in preheated 375° F oven for 35–45 minutes for rare, or until internal temperature is 140° F. For medium meat, cook until internal temperature is 165° F. For well done, cook until internal temperature is 180° F. When roast is done, place on serving tray and carve. Pour some of the sauce on top and garnish with mushrooms. Surround tray with parsley, watercress, and sliced oranges with currant jelly.

Party Onions

5 lb. small or medium white onions
1½ cups butter
1 cup flour
⅓ cup brown sugar
5 cups water
1 tbsp. + 2 tsp. salt
1 tbsp. + 2 tsp. worcestershire
1½ tsp. paprika
1 cup slivered almonds, toasted

Cover onions and cook in a small amount of boiling, salted water until tender. Drain well. Arrange in 2-qt. casserole. In saucepan, melt butter and blend in flour. Stir in water, brown sugar, salt, worcestershire, and pepper. Cook until mixture thickens slightly and bubbles. Pour over onions. Sprinkle with paprika. Cover and bake at 375° F for 20 minutes. Before serving, sprinkle with toasted almonds.

Petit Pois in Tomato Cups

10–12 tomatoes
20-oz. frozen bag petit pois

Scoop out enough pulp from tomatoes to hold peas. Cook peas according to package directions, adding a little of the pulp to the water. Put tomatoes in roasting pan in oven for 10 minutes or more until tomato is hot but not mushy and still holds its shape. Fill with peas.

Sesame Rolls

2 packages refrigerated Pillsbury crescent rolls
1 cup butter
½ cup chopped parsley
⅛ tsp. thyme
sesame seeds

Parsley Butter
Soften 1 cup of butter and mix in parsley and thyme.

Take dough out of packages without unrolling it. Slice dough into ½″ rounds. Spread parsley butter thickly over bottom of cookie pan. Place rolls in pan and sprinkle with sesame seeds; let stand 1 hour at room temperature; cook according to directions on package. Can be made ahead and reheated at last minute.

Cointreau Soufflé

¾ cup orange juice
¼ cup lemon juice
2 tbsp. unflavored gelatin
grated peel of 2 oranges and 1 lemon
⅓ cup cointreau
6 eggs, separated
2 cups sugar
½ tsp. salt
2 cups heavy cream
grated peel of 1 orange for garnish

Grate rind of 2 oranges and lemon and squeeze juice. Sprinkle gelatin into ½ cup of orange juice and set aside. In a saucepan, put the grated peel, remaining ¼ cup orange juice, lemon juice, cointreau, 6 egg yolks, 1¼ cups sugar, and salt. Beat until fluffy. Stir over low heat until mixture coats back of spoon. Remove from heat and stir in softened gelatin–orange juice mixture, stirring until gelatin dissolves. Place in refrigerator to cool for 20 minutes.

Beat egg whites to soft peaks. Beat in remaining ¾ cup sugar, 1 tsp. at a time, and beat until stiff and glossy. Beat 2 cups of heavy cream until soft peaks form. Fold in egg whites, then turn whipped cream into egg-yolk custard and pour into 6-cup soufflé dish with waxed paper collar. Place in refrigerator and chill overnight.

Garnish with grated orange peel.

★

Springtime Fare

(serves 8)

★ VICHYSOISSE

★ ROAST LEG OF LAMB WITH VEGETABLES

MINT SAUCE

BIBB LETTUCE AND CHIVES WITH

★ ITALIAN DRESSING

BRIE AND PORT SALUT CHEESES

WATER BISCUITS

FRESH APPLES, GRAPES AND PEARS

★

Vichysoisse

4 cups cubed potatoes
1 cup sliced celery
1 cup chopped onion
2 cups chicken broth
2 tsp. salt
1 cup milk
1 cup heavy cream
3 tbsp. butter
⅛ tsp. pepper

Cook potatoes, celery, onion, and salt in broth in large kettle until vegetables are tender. Put undrained vegetables through food mill. Pour back into kettle. Add remaining ingredients for a few minutes to mix. Chill. Sprinkle with chives.

Roast Leg of Lamb with Vegetables

6½-lb. spring leg of lamb, semiboneless
garlic salt
rosemary leaves
2 lb. potatoes, peeled
1–2 lb. small pearl onions
1 lb. baby carrots

Preheat oven to 400° F. Make sure tough membrane covering lamb has been removed. Rub meat with garlic salt on all sides. Add rosemary to same areas. Set meat in shallow roasting pan until it reaches room temperature. Cook at 400° F for 15 minutes to sear juices. Reduce heat to 350° F and continue cooking (30 minutes to the pound for medium). Occasionally add boiling water to make juices.

Parboil carrots and potatoes and pearl onions. Approximately 1 hour before serving, add onions, potatoes, and carrots to roast. Turn vegetables frequently for even browning. At serving time, remove meat to platter and surround with vegetables.

Italian Dressing

½ cup olive and peanut oil mixed
¼ cup Tarragon vinegar
¼ tsp. of each of the following:
    parsley flakes
    tarragon
    thyme
    dried mustard
    sweet marjoram
    paprika
    sugar
    salt
juice of lemon
freshly ground pepper to taste

Pour all ingredients in a bowl and mix with fork about 1 hour before serving.

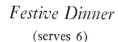

Festive Dinner

(serves 6)

★ LOIN OF PORK WITH GLAZED APRICOTS

NEW POTATOES

★ TANGY SPINACH SALAD

★ FESTIVE APPLE PIE

Loin of Pork with Glazed Apricots

6-lb. loin of pork, trimmed
¼ cup oil
2 carrots, sliced
1 medium onion, chopped
1 stalk celery, sliced
¼ tsp. dried sage
1 bay leaf
1 tbsp. salt
1 tsp. pepper
1 cup brown sauce
1 cup dry white wine
1 lb. dried apricots
½ cup honey

Brown Sauce

Melt 1½ tbsp. butter in a heavy skillet. Remove from heat and add 1½ tbsp. flour. Blend well, return to heat, and cook over low heat, stirring occasionally until it is a good brown color. Add 1 can consommé or beef stock slowly. Bring to a boil and cook for 5 minutes, stirring constantly. Lower heat and simmer gently for 30–40 minutes, stirring occasionally. Skim off fat and season to taste with salt and pepper. Makes one cup.

Cook pork in roasting pan with oil for 10 minutes at 450° F to sear. Add vegetables and let them brown. Add herbs and seasonings, pour in wine and brown sauce. Cover the pan and put in a 300° F oven for 2½ to 3 hours. Remove loin. Meanwhile, poach apricots in one quart water for 20 minutes. Strain. Put apricots and honey into a saucepan over low heat until glazed. Arrange over loin of pork. Strain sauce from roasting pan and pour around loin.

Tangy Spinach Salad

    1 lb. fresh spinach
    ¾ lb. bacon, fried and crumbled

Dressing

    2 tbsp. bacon drippings
    ¼ cup red wine vinegar
    3 tbsp. tarragon vinegar
    1 to 2 cloves garlic, crushed
    ⅔ cup olive oil
    1 tsp. worcestershire
    1 tsp. salt
    ¼ tsp. pepper

Mix all ingredients together. Toss with bacon over spinach. This is best when dressing is made a day ahead.

Festive Apple Pie

    unbaked 9″ pie shell
    2 tbsp. flour
    ⅛ tsp. salt
    ¾ cup sugar
    1 unbeaten egg
    1 cup sour cream
    1 tsp. vanilla
    ¼ tsp. nutmeg
    2 cups diced, peeled apples (winesap or Jonathan are best)

Topping

    ⅓ cup sugar
    ⅓ cup flour
    1 tsp. cinnamon
    ¼ cup butter
    apple slices (optional)

Sift together flour, salt, and sugar. Add egg, sour cream, vanilla, and nutmeg. Beat to a smooth, thin batter. Blend in apples and pour into pie shell. Bake at 400° F for 15 minutes, then turn down oven to 350° F for 30 minutes.

Topping

While pie bakes, mix together sugar, flour, cinnamon, and butter until crumbly.

Remove pie from the oven, sprinkle topping over the top, then brown for 10 minutes at 400° F. Decorate with apple slices (dipped in lemon juice to prevent browning) if you wish.

A Touch of Paris
(serves 4)

★ FRENCH SALAD

★ DRUNKEN SCALLOPS

BUTTERMILK BISCUITS

ASPARAGUS WITH HOLLANDAISE SAUCE

PEACH MELBA

French Salad

1 head escarole
¼ lb. fresh spinach
1 can mandarin oranges
½ red onion, thinly sliced
¼ lb. bleu cheese, crumbled

Combine ingredients and toss with favorite French dressing.

Drunken Scallops

1½ to 2 lb. sea scallops
1 cup flour
½ cup chopped fresh parsley
4 slices cooked bacon, crumbled
3 shallots, diced
1 large clove of garlic, minced
1 tsp. dried oregano
olive oil
butter
1 cup dry white wine (use rest of wine for serving)

Wash and thoroughly dry scallops, then roll in flour to coat. Heat small, equal amounts of oil and butter in skillet. Cook all ingredients except wine for 4–5 minutes, stirring to prevent sticking. Add more oil or butter if needed. Remove scallops to serving dish and keep warm. Add wine to the skillet, stirring to loosen all scallop bits, and boil until liquid has been reduced to half the volume. Pour over scallops. Season with salt and pepper and serve.

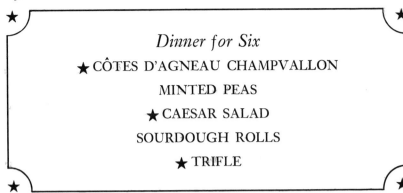

Côtes d'Agneau Champvallon

12 rib lamb chops
3 onions, thinly sliced
4 potatoes, thinly sliced
3 cups consommé
½ cup white wine
2 cloves garlic, crushed
bouquet garni of parsley, with 1 bay leaf, thyme, and chopped
    parsley

Season chops with salt, brown lightly in butter. Remove chops and drippings. Add butter and cook sliced onions until soft, but not brown. Mix raw potatoes with onions and season with salt, thyme, and crushed garlic. Add bouquet garni. Remove from pan. Combine chop drippings and onions and cook until thickened and light brown. Add 3 cups consommé and wine. Dissolve drippings and remove from fire. In a baking dish, alternately layer onion and potatoes with chops. Add pan liquids. Bring to a boil over stove, then put in 375° F oven for 45 minutes. Garnish with parsley.

Caesar Salad

2 medium garlic cloves
1 tsp. salt
6 tbsp. oil
2 tbsp. wine vinegar
1 tbsp. fresh lemon juice
½ tsp. worcestershire

1 tsp. dry mustard
½ tsp. salt
1 tsp. black pepper
4 fillets of anchovies, cut up in small pieces (or 2 tsp. anchovy
    paste)
1 tbsp. Parmesan cheese
1 lb. cold, crisp romaine lettuce
1 coddled egg
24 or more small croutons

Into large wooden salad bowl, place 2 medium cloves of garlic and salt. Crush with fork and rub bowl until bowl is well flavored with garlic. May discard garlic and salt or leave in bowl. Add oil and beat rapidly with fork until thick. Add wine vinegar and lemon juice slowly. Beat until thoroughly blended with oil. Add worcestershire, mustard, salt (less if first salt has been left in bowl), pepper, anchovies, and Parmesan cheese. Beat until well blended. Add lettuce in small pieces. Toss. Add egg and mix well. Add croutons and toss again. Serve at once.

Trifle

3 eggs
½ cup sugar
2 cups milk
1 tsp. almond extract
1 sponge cake or 4 packages ladyfingers
¾ to 1 cup dry sherry
fresh (1 qt.) or canned (1 lb., 13 oz.) fruit (use your favorites:
    canned peaches, crushed pineapple, mandarin oranges,
    bing cherries, strawberries, blueberries, raspberries)
1 cup whipped cream
toasted slivered almonds

Beat eggs, sugar, and a dash of salt in top of double boiler. Stir in milk. Cook, stirring constantly, until mixture has thickened. Add almond extract. Chill.

Break the cake into bite-size pieces and arrange half of them on the bottom of serving dish. Sprinkle the cake with half of the sherry. Arrange half of the fruit the same way. Spoon on half of the custard. Repeat the process. Top with whipped cream and almonds. Chill for several hours before serving.

★

Family Dinner

(serves 4–6)

★ VEAL STEW

BUTTERED PARSLIED NOODLES

★ BENSON BROCCOLI

★ LACY OATMEAL COOKIES AND SHERBET

★

Veal Stew

    2 lb. veal cubes
    3 onions
    1 clove garlic, minced
    1 package beef bouillon
    tomato juice: a little less than 1 cup
    green pepper chunks
    mushrooms

Brown veal in skillet. Add remaining ingredients, except for mushrooms and green pepper. Cook ½ hour. Add pepper and mushrooms and cook 15 minutes longer.

Benson Broccoli

    1 can mushroom soup
    ¾ cup mayonnaise
    1 cup N.Y. State cheese
    2 eggs, beaten
    2 packages broccoli, thawed
    salt and pepper

Mix all ingredients together. Cover with bread crumbs. Bake at 350° F until crumbs are browned.

Lacy Oatmeal Cookies

1 cup quick oats
1 cup sugar
½ cup margarine (*not* butter)
4 tbsp. flour
½ tsp. salt
1 tsp. vanilla
1 egg
1½ tsp. baking powder

Melt margarine. Add all ingredients to margarine. Cover cookie sheet with foil. Drop ⅓ tsp. of mixture on cookie sheet 2 or 3 inches apart. Bake 10 minutes at 350° F. Watch carefully. Allow to cool on foil. Peel foil off cookies. Use new foil for each batch. Makes about 60.

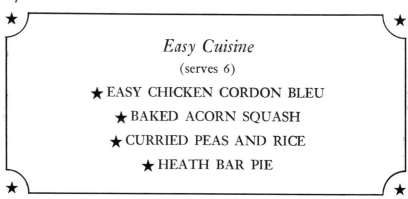

Easy Cuisine

(serves 6)

★ EASY CHICKEN CORDON BLEU

★ BAKED ACORN SQUASH

★ CURRIED PEAS AND RICE

★ HEATH BAR PIE

Easy Chicken Cordon Bleu

12 boned chicken breasts
12 slices of thinly sliced ham
12 chunks of Swiss cheese (large enough to be rolled inside each breast)
2 cans cream of celery soup, undiluted

Pound breasts until thin. Place a slice of ham and a piece of cheese on each breast. Roll each piece and secure with a toothpick. Place rolled breasts in a shallow pan which has been lined with foil. Stir the 2 cans of soup until creamy. Pour over all and bake for 1 to 1½ hours at 325° F or until the breasts are tender and sauce bubbles. Do not overcook.

Baked Acorn Squash

3 acorn squashes
6 tbsp. butter
salt
6 tsp. brown sugar
dash of cinnamon

Cut squashes in half; do not pare. Remove seeds. In center of each half, put 1 tbsp. butter, sprinkle with salt and cinnamon, then add 1 tsp. of brown sugar. Cover bottom of 9″ × 13″ pan with water, place squash in water right side up and bake at 350° F for 1½ hours.

Curried Peas and Rice

two 10-oz. packages frozen peas
1½ cups cooked rice
½ cup mayonnaise
1 tbsp. curry
pepper and salt to taste

Cook peas and rice according to directions. Drain peas and mix with rice. Refrigerate vegetables before adding remaining ingredients. Add additional mayonnaise and curry if needed. Season to taste. Serve on lettuce leaves.

Heath Bar Pie

2 packages ladyfingers
7 Heath Bars, regular size
1 large container Cool Whip

Split ladyfingers and fit sunflower fashion in pie plate (bottom and sides). Mash Heath Bars (you can use bottom of pop bottle as masher) and add them to container of Cool Whip. Pile half of filling on ladyfingers, then put on another layer of ladyfinger halves and spread on balance of filling. Let the pie chill in refrigerator at least 6 hours before serving.

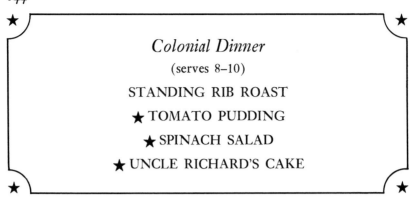

Colonial Dinner

(serves 8–10)

STANDING RIB ROAST

★ TOMATO PUDDING

★ SPINACH SALAD

★ UNCLE RICHARD'S CAKE

Tomato Pudding

12 slices bread, cubed
½ lb. butter, melted
4 small cans tomato puree
2 cups brown sugar

Cut bread into cubes and put into baking dish in warm oven to dry (or toast lightly). Melt butter and stir into cubes. Simmer tomato puree with brown sugar until sugar is melted. Pour over bread and bake in 350° F oven 20–30 minutes. Serve hot.

Spinach Salad

three 10-oz. packages fresh spinach
6 hard-boiled eggs
¾ to 1 lb. bacon, crisply cooked and crumbled
red onion, sliced thinly

Dressing

½ cup sugar
1 tsp. salt
1 tbsp. cornstarch
2 eggs
¾ cup cider vinegar
¼ cup water

Mix together sugar, salt, and cornstarch. Add eggs, well beaten. Gradually add vinegar and water and cook in double boiler until thick. When using, mix with equal amount of mayonnaise. Toss over spinach salad.

Uncle Richard's Cake

Cake

>   ¼ lb. butter
>   1 cup sugar
>   4 eggs
>   1 cup cake flour
>   1-lb. can Hershey's chocolate syrup
>   ½ tsp. vanilla

Cream butter and sugar. Add eggs one at a time and beat well. Add syrup and flour alternately. Add vanilla. Bake in a greased and floured tube pan at 350° F for 45 minutes or until it tests for doneness. Keeps well because it is moist.

Frosting

>   2 tbsp. softened butter
>   1 square melted chocolate or 2 oz. melted chocolate bits
>   1 cup sifted confectioners' sugar
>   ⅛ cup coffee
>   ¼ tsp. vanilla
>   2 tsp. marshmallow fluff

Mix all ingredients together. It is a thin frosting.

★

Friday Night Dinner

(serves 6)

★ CHILLED TOMATO SOUP

★ DEVILED FISH FILLETS

PEA PODS AND CARROTS

STRAW POTATOES

★ GLAZED STRAWBERRY TARTS

★

Chilled Tomato Soup

4 large fresh tomatoes
2 small onions, or 1 medium onion
1 large garlic clove, crushed
1 tsp. salt
¼ tsp. ground pepper
½ to 1 tsp. dill
2 tbsp. tomato paste
¼ cup cold water
1 cup chicken stock
croutons (optional)

Peel and slice tomatoes into saucepan. Add onion, garlic, and next 5 ingredients. Simmer 15 minutes. Put into container of blender and cover. Turn on *high*. Uncover, reduce to *low*, and add chicken stock. Cover and turn to *high* for a few seconds more. Chill and serve garnished with a lemon slice and chopped parsley. Pass croutons. If preferred, this soup may be served hot.

Deviled Fish Fillets

2½ to 3 lb. thick sole or flounder fillets
½ tsp. salt
¼ cup sour cream
¼ cup mayonnaise
4 tsp. Dijon mustard
1 tsp. dried onion flakes
lemon, to squeeze over fish

Preheat oven to 500° F. Wash fillets and dry with paper towels. Arrange fish in a single layer, slightly overlapping, in a greased, shallow baking dish, or on heat-proof platter. Sprinkle with salt and squeeze on lemon juice. Mix sour cream with mayonnaise, mustard, and onion. Spread evenly over top of fish. Bake, uncovered, 15 minutes, or until sauce starts to brown. Garnish with lemon slices and parsley.

Glazed Strawberry Tarts

Pastry

> 2 cups flour
> 4 tbsp. sugar
> ⅛ tsp. baking powder
> 5 tbsp. chilled butter
> 2 tbsp. chilled margarine or lard
> 1 egg beaten with 1 tsp. water
> ½ tsp. vanilla

Mix flour, sugar, butter, margarine, and baking powder together until mixture has small flakes. Add egg and vanilla and knead into ball. Chill for several hours. Then roll out pastry and cut into rounds to fit into muffin tin shells. Bake at 375° F for about 15 minutes, or until lightly browned.

Filling

> 1 pt. strawberries
> 1 cup red currant jelly
> 2 tbsp. sugar

Combine sugar and jelly in a saucepan and boil until thickened.

Fill cooled pastry shells with fresh, cleaned strawberries and pour the cooked glaze over them.

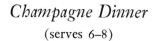

Champagne Dinner
(serves 6–8)

★ CHICKEN IN CHAMPAGNE SAUCE
LONG GRAIN AND WILD RICE
★ ARTICHOKE-STUFFED TOMATOES
★ NORMANDY CHOCOLATE MOUSSE

Chicken in Champagne Sauce

two 6-oz. packages Uncle Ben's long grain and wild rice
6 whole chicken breasts: split, boned, and skinned
½ cup flour
salt and pepper
½ tsp. ginger
½ cup butter
2 onions, quartered
2 carrots, quartered
1 bay leaf
2 splits champagne or 2 cups dry white wine
2 cups heavy cream
two 8-oz. cans green grapes, or fresh if available

Shake chicken pieces in bag with seasoned flour, using all the flour, salt, pepper, and ginger. Brown slowly in butter about 5 minutes each side. Add onions, bay leaf, and champagne or wine. Cover pan and simmer 25 minutes, until chicken is tender. Discard bay leaf, onions, and carrots. Prepare rice according to package directions. Arrange rice on platter, place chicken on top. Add cream and grapes to sauce. Heat without boiling. Spoon over chicken.

Artichoke-Stuffed Tomatoes

For each serving, scoop out hole in tomato large enough to hold artichoke heart. Sprinkle with salt and sugar. Place marinated artichoke in center. Broil until tender.

Normandy Chocolate Mousse

1 lb. dark sweet chocolate, cut up
2 oz. bitter chocolate, cut up
7 tbsp. strong coffee
2 tbsp. rum or Kirsch
5 eggs, separated
2 oz. sweet butter
1 cup heavy cream
2 dozen ladyfingers, split
whipped cream
reserved chocolate, shredded

Place both chocolates and coffee in heavy pan over low heat, reserving a small amount of sweet chocolate for garnish. Stir until chocolate is melted. Add rum or Kirsch. Remove from heat. Add egg yolks, one at a time. Add butter bit by bit. Beat the cream over a bowl of ice until thick. Add slowly to chocolate mixture. Beat the egg whites until stiff and fold in. Lightly butter a 9″ Charlotte mold and line with ladyfingers. Fill with mousse and chill in freezer overnight. Allow to warm slightly at room temperature, unmold onto serving plate, and decorate with whipped cream and shredded chocolate.

MT. HOLLY
QUAKER MEETING
HOUSE:

International Cuisine

Mount Holly Meeting House in Mount Holly, New Jersey

MOUNT HOLLY is a Quaker Meeting House which was founded in 1776 and is located in New Jersey. The meeting house was in the possession of Sir Henry Clinton and his army, who used the structure for the headquarters of the commissary department and a receptacle for their military stores in 1778.

Later the meeting house also performed its part in the great struggle of the infant nation, as the host for several sessions of the New Jersey State Legislature in November, 1779.

The New Jersey Quakers resembled their Pennsylvania neighbors in the way they spent their lives. They were alike in their farming techniques, the arrangement of rooms in their homes, and the types of implements used in cooking. The Quaker lady was a typically Colonial American in that she spent her days cleaning the home, cooking for her family, and raising her children [Ed: Some things never change!!] However, Sunday in the Colonies was set aside as a day of rest and communion with God at the church of one's choice. In the Society of Friends, any recreation time was usually spent attending meetings and the yearly meeting served as a vacation for the women.

A balanced life was the Quaker ideal of living. They saw the divine potential in everyman and thus asserted that one must treat his neighbor as a Friend. This principle led them, as today, to avoid war and cultivate the arts and advantages of peace.

The Quakers were considered "semi-epicures," who enjoyed the best food, yet practiced moderation in drinking. One typical "first day's meal" at a rural home (most American Quakers were farmers) consisted of bread and butter, smoked beef, apples, and cider. The women drank tea!

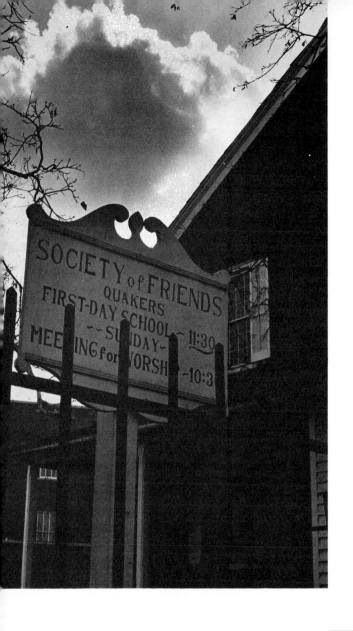

Early American Repast

(serves 6–8)

★ CHICKEN LIVERS

BUTTERED TOAST POINTS

★ BROCCOLI CASSEROLE

★ APPLE CRISP

Chicken Livers

12 slices bacon
½ cup butter
1 large onion, chopped
8-oz. can tomato sauce
1 tbsp. Dijon mustard
chopped parsley
marjoram
thyme
paprika
chili powder
ginger
2 lb. chicken livers
flour for dredging
salt
freshly ground pepper
½ cup brandy

Cook bacon, crumble, and set aside. Pour off the bacon fat, add 2 tbsp. butter and the onion. Cook until golden. Add the tomato sauce and mustard, and a dash each of the next 6 ingredients. Add the bacon, and mix over low heat. Set aside and keep warm. Remove the fatty membrane from the livers. Season the flour with salt and pepper, place in a bag, and toss the livers in to coat. Put the remaining butter in a heavy skillet and cook the livers over medium heat. Cook for approximately 15 minutes, turning frequently, and sprinkle with some brandy during cooking. Before serving, add the bacon mixture and the rest of the brandy. Spoon over buttered toast points.

Broccoli Casserole

4 cups fresh broccoli, cooked and chopped
1 can golden mushroom soup
¾ cup sour cream
2-oz. jar sliced pimentos
1 tsp. salt
1 small can water chestnuts, chopped
½ cup grated cheddar cheese

Combine all ingredients except the cheese. Place in a greased 2-qt. casserole and sprinkle the cheese on top. Bake at 350° F for 30 minutes.

Apple Crisp

4 cups apples, pared and sliced
3 cups brown sugar
2 cups flour
1 cup butter, softened
2 tsp. cinnamon

Mix 1½ cups of the sugar into apples. Blend balance of ingredients with fork. Place apples in large, buttered pan. Press topping over apples. Bake at 375° F for ½ hour or until apples are tender.

Italian Supper
(serves 8)
MINESTRONE SOUP

BOSTON LETTUCE

WITH ★ SIS'S SALAD DRESSING

★ BAKED LASAGNA

CHEESE ROLLS

★ TORTONI

Sis's Salad Dressing

2 cloves garlic
¼ cup sugar
¼ cup salad oil
¼ cup vinegar
2 tsp. salt
bleu cheese

Mince garlic and add sugar, salad oil, vinegar, and salt. Whisk together and pour over Boston lettuce. Sprinkle grated bleu cheese on top to taste.

Baked Lasagna

1 package lasagna noodles
3 tbsp. salad oil
salt, pepper, oregano, garlic powder, celery salt

Meatballs
1½ lb. ground chuck
1 onion, chopped
1 tsp. salt
1 egg
1 tbsp. oregano
48-oz. jar meatless spaghetti sauce

Cheese Filling
>   1 lb. ricotta cheese
>   ½ lb. mozzarella, grated
>   2 eggs, beaten
>   1 tsp. salt
>   pinch of pepper
>   pepperoni
>   Parmesan cheese

Boil the noodles, following package directions, adding 1 tbsp. of the oil to the water to avoid sticking.

Combine the ingredients for the meatballs in a large bowl and form into meatballs approximately ½″ in diameter. Brown them in the remaining oil. In a large pan, combine the browned meatballs, spaghetti sauce, and seasonings to taste. Simmer for 10 minutes (prepare 1 day ahead for better flavor). In a large bowl, combine the ingredients for the cheese filling.

Grease a 13″ × 9″ × 2″ (or larger) baking dish. (Have another dish ready in case of overflow.) Place some sauce on the bottom of the dish. Line the dish with a layer of noodles, so the ends extend up the sides of the dish. Follow with a layer of cheese filling, then sauce. Repeat the layers until all the ingredients are used, ending with sauce. Top with thinly sliced pepperoni. Sprinkle with Parmesan cheese. (May be frozen or made a day ahead.) Bake unfrozen at 375° F for 40 minutes, frozen for 1 hour, 15 minutes, until hot and bubbly.

Tortoni

>   1 egg white
>   1 tbsp. instant coffee
>   ½ tsp. salt
>   1 tsp. vanilla
>   ⅛ tsp. almond extract
>   ¼ cup sugar
>   1 cup heavy cream
>   ¼ cup toasted, slivered almonds

Combine egg white, coffee, and salt. Beat until stiff. Add vanilla, almond extract, and sugar to the cream. Beat until stiff. Fold in nuts and egg white mixture. Put in paper cups, sprinkle with a few more nuts, and freeze.

★

Polynesian Supper

(serves 8)

★ SWEET AND SOUR MEAT LOAF

★ VEGETABLE SALAD MOLD

BAKED POTATO

★ CRANBERRY–APPLE CRISP

WITH SOUR CREAM SAUCE

★

Sweet and Sour Meat Loaf

8-oz. can tomato sauce
¼ cup brown sugar
¼ cup vinegar
1 tsp. mustard
1 egg, beaten
1 onion, minced
¼ cup crushed crackers
2 lb. ground chuck
1¼ tsp. salt
¼ tsp. pepper

Mix the tomato sauce with the sugar, vinegar, and mustard. Combine the egg, onion, crackers, ground chuck, salt, pepper, and half of the tomato sauce mixture. Shape into a loaf or cook in a ring mold. Bake at 375° F for 1 hour. Pour on the remaining sauce when serving.

Vegetable Salad Mold

1-qt., 14-oz. can tomato juice
1 package gelatin
3 small boxes lemon jello
3–5 dashes Tabasco
2 tsp. worcestershire
6 grated carrots
5–8 scallions, chopped
4 celery stalks, chopped
1 avocado, peeled and chopped
½ tsp. salt
3 tbsp. lemon juice

Bring gelatin to a boil in 1 cup of tomato juice. Add 2 cups of tomato juice and pour in the lemon jello. Add the remaining tomato juice and jell until slightly thickened. Add the rest of the ingredients, pour into a mold, and chill until firm.

Cranberry–Apple Crisp with Sour Cream Sauce

3 cups cranberries
3 cups tart apples, sliced
2 tbsp. brown sugar
⅓ cup butter, melted
1 tsp. cinnamon

Topping
1 cup flour
¾ cup sugar
1 tsp. baking powder
1 large egg

Sour Cream Sauce
1 pt. sour cream
1 tsp. sugar
1 tsp. vanilla

Place fruit in a greased 9″ × 13″ baking dish and top with brown sugar. Mix topping ingredients with a fork; sprinkle on top of fruit. Drizzle with melted butter and cinnamon. Bake at 375° F for 30 minutes. Combine the sauce ingredients and chill until used. Serve warm or cold.

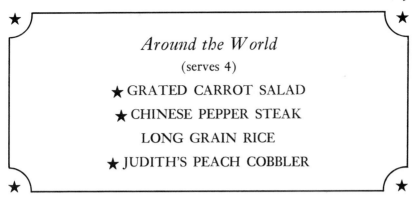

Around the World
(serves 4)

★ GRATED CARROT SALAD

★ CHINESE PEPPER STEAK

LONG GRAIN RICE

★ JUDITH'S PEACH COBBLER

Grated Carrot Salad

1½ bunches carrots
½ to ¾ cup mayonnaise
¼ cup sour cream
½ cup raisins
1 tbsp. ginger marmalade
dash of cinnamon
dash of nutmeg

Scrape and grate the carrots. Mix sour cream and mayonnaise until smooth, and add the rest of the ingredients. Toss dressing with the carrots, and serve on lettuce leaves.

Chinese Pepper Steak

4 tbsp. olive oil
⅛ tsp. garlic powder
1 tsp. salt
½ tsp. pepper
1 tsp. ginger
1 lb. flank steak, cut into bite-size pieces
4 tbsp. soya sauce
½ tsp. sugar
1 can French-style green beans
2 tomatoes, coarsely chopped
1–2 green peppers, chopped
1 tbsp. cornstarch

In large skillet, heat oil with next four ingredients. Add the steak and brown lightly for 2 minutes. Add the soya sauce and sugar, cover and cook 2 minutes longer. Add beans, tomatoes, and peppers, then cover and cook briskly for 5 minutes. Blend the cornstarch in ¼ cup cold water and add. Cook, stirring until sauce thickens. Serve over rice.

Judith's Peach Cobbler

¾ cup flour
dash of salt
2 tbsp. baking powder
2 cups sugar
¾ cup milk
½ cup butter
2 cups fresh peaches, sliced

Sift flour, salt, and baking powder. Mix with 1 cup of the sugar. Slowly stir in milk. Melt butter in an 8″ × 8″ × 2″ pan. Pour batter over. *Do not stir.* Combine the peaches and the rest of the sugar. Carefully spoon over the batter. Bake at 350° F for 1 hour.

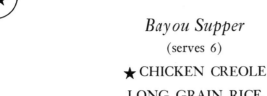

Bayou Supper

(serves 6)

★ CHICKEN CREOLE

LONG GRAIN RICE

SAUTÉED ZUCCHINI AND ONIONS

★ CREAM CHEESE PIE

Chicken Creole

3½ to 4 lb. chicken
salt and pepper
2 tbsp. butter or margarine
1 cup sliced onions
2 tbsp. flour
2 cups cooked or canned tomatoes
2 cloves garlic, minced
1 tsp. thyme
2 tsp. minced parsley
2 bay leaves
2 cups chopped green pepper
1 cup boiling water
1¼ tsp. salt
¼ tsp. pepper

Disjoint chicken and bone. Rub with salt and pepper. Heat butter and add chicken. Brown slowly for 5 minutes. Cut into bite-size pieces. Add onions and brown. Add flour, tomatoes, garlic, thyme, parsley, and bay leaves. Cover pan and simmer over low heat. Stir occasionally. When gravy is reduced by half, add green pepper and boiling water. Simmer until chicken is tender. Add salt and pepper, and more water if needed. Serve over long grain rice.

Cream Cheese Pie

Crust

2 cups graham cracker crumbs
½ cup sugar
½ cup butter, melted

Bottom Layer

two 8-oz. packages cream cheese
⅔ cup sugar
2 eggs
1 tsp. vanilla

Top Layer

1 cup sour cream
2 tbsp. sugar

Combine ingredients for the crust and press into a 9″ or 10″ pie plate. Mix the ingredients for the bottom layer, pour into the crust, and bake at 375° F for 15 minutes. Let stand for half an hour.

Mix ingredients for the top layer, add, and bake at 425° F for 10 minutes. Chill.

All-American Supper
(serves 8)

★ SLOPPY JOES

CORN ON THE COB

★ FOUR-BEAN SALAD

★ LEMON CHESS PIE

Sloppy Joes

1 cup soft bread crumbs
¼ cup tomato juice
1 lb. ground beef
½ tsp. pepper
2 tbsp. sugar
2 tbsp. vinegar
½ cup catsup
2 tbsp. water
2 tbsp. worcestershire sauce
8 hamburger rolls

Brown beef and crumbs in small amount of fat. Add the rest of the ingredients and simmer 10 min. Spread on bun halves. Put buns and meat in individual pieces of foil and bake for 30 minutes, until heated through and roll top is toasted.

Four-Bean Salad

16-oz. can kidney beans
16-oz. can chick peas (Garbanzo beans)
16-oz. can Blue Lake cut green beans
16-oz. can yellow wax beans
2 sweet onions, sliced
¼ cup sugar
⅔ cup tarragon vinegar
⅓ cup salad oil
salt
freshly ground pepper

Drain all beans thoroughly and place in large glass bowl. Add sliced onions. Mix sugar, vinegar, salad oil, salt, and pepper. Pour over drained beans and onions. Cover and refrigerate overnight.

Lemon Chess Pie

½ stick butter
2 cups sugar
¼ cup white cornmeal
4 eggs
½ cup lemon juice
9″ uncooked pie shell

Cream butter, sugar, and cornmeal. Beat in eggs, one at a time. Add lemon juice. Pour into crust and bake at 350° F for about 40 minutes, until brown on top.

Chinese Supper
(serves 4)

SLICED AVOCADO

WITH ORANGE AND GRAPEFRUIT SECTIONS

★ FRENCH DRESSING

★ PORK CHOW MEIN

RICE

CHOW MEIN NOODLES

SNOW PEAS

★ PUMPKIN LOAF

French Dressing

1 cup corn oil or peanut oil
5 tbsp. wine or apple cider vinegar
1 tsp. dry mustard
1 tsp. salt
¼ tsp. paprika
½ cup sugar
3 tbsp. lemon juice

Mix in jar in given order. Float the half lemon in dressing for flavor and marinating. Refrigerate until serving over fruit salad.

Pork Chow Mein

3 tbsp. oil
1 lb. pork, cut into thin strips
3 cups celery, cut diagonally
1 cup onion, sliced
1 cup fresh mushrooms, sliced
2½ tbsp. cornstarch
1 can condensed beef broth
¼ cup soya sauce
1 tbsp. brown gravy sauce (optional)
1-lb. can bean sprouts, drained
5-oz. can water chestnuts, drained and sliced

Cook pork in 1 tbsp. hot oil for approximately 10 minutes, then remove. Cook celery, onion, and mushrooms in remaining 2 tbsp. oil until crisp and tender, 2–3 minutes, stirring often. Blend cornstarch in ¼ cup water. Add beef broth and soya sauce (and gravy sauce, if desired). Stir into vegetables. Add meat, bean sprouts, and water chestnuts. Heat until thickened, but do not overcook. Serve over rice. Top with chow mein noodles.

Pumpkin Loaf

1 cup fresh pumpkin
3 cups sugar
3 cups flour
1 tsp. cinnamon
1 tsp. nutmeg
½ tsp. salt
2 tsp. baking soda
1 cup oil
⅔ cup cold water
4 eggs

Sift dry ingredients, then stir in the rest. Grease and flour three 1-lb. coffee cans. Pour batter into the cans and bake at 350° F for 1 hour. Store in the refrigerator.

VALLEY FORGE
BAKE HOUSE:
Men in the Kitchen

The Bake House at Valley Forge

VALLEY FORGE was General George Washington's headquarters west of Philadelphia during the winter of 1777–1778. Today, this site continues to remind everyone of the courage and patriotism of Washington and his troops. He chose Valley Forge for his headquarters because he wished to be as near as possible to Philadelphia. At the same time, he was carefully establishing himself in a readily defensible position so he could pose a constant threat to General Howe.

The troops began to set up camp the day after Thanksgiving. The men were divided into parties of twelve, each to build their own cabin. The cabins were sixteen feet long by fourteen feet wide, with walls six and a half feet high. Clay filled the gaps between the logs. The officers' cabins, which were very similar, stood in line behind those of their men.

Food was normally issued directly to the individual Continental soldier. At Valley Forge the optimal rations included a pound and a half of flour or bread, one pound of beef or fish, three-fourths pound of pork, and a gill of whiskey or spirits. Naturally these raw provisions varied according to the quantity and type of foods available in camp. Sometimes they were reduced and hunger became a real factor.

It was the job of the soldiers to cook for themselves. A bakery was set up to provide bread instead of flour, but the preparation of everyday foods was left to the skill of the men. Cooking utensils were distributed as a part of normal camp equipage, hopefully including a set for every six or eight men. Such a group—or mess—would get together and select the best individual cooks among them to prepare the meals for the others. In order for the soldiers to do their cooking, they were issued camp kettles. Provisions, they were told, "ought always to be boiled or roasted, never fried, baked or broiled, which modes are very unhealthy." The men were also taught to use vinegar freely as an aid to health.

Cooking utensils
issued to the
Continental soldier

Candlewax heating in the
iron pot in the bake oven

Candlemaking apparatus

West side of Valley Forge landmark

Shredded Wheat Bread

2 cups boiling water
2 tbsp. shortening
2 tsp. salt
⅓ cup molasses
2 large shredded wheat biscuits
1 package dry yeast
¼ cup lukewarm water
5 cups flour

Mix together boiling water, shortening, salt, molasses, and shredded wheat. Dissolve yeast in the lukewarm water and add to above. Add flour. Turn out onto floured board. Knead 8 minutes, adding more flour until stickiness is gone. Grease mixing bowl. Put in bread. Cover with clean damp dish towel.

Allow to rise 2 hours in warm place until double in bulk. Pound down, then let rise again 1 hour. Turn out onto board. Let it relax 10 minutes. Shape into 2 loaves and put into greased loaf pans. Brush top with butter. Bake at 400° F for 45–50 minutes.

Makes super toast.

Simpson's Caesar Salad
(serves 4–6)

2 bunches Romaine lettuce
1 can flat anchovies
1 clove garlic
1 egg yolk
1 tsp. dry mustard
1½ tbsp. lemon juice
3 tbsp. olive oil
Tabasco to taste
couple dashes worcestershire sauce
¼ cup Parmesan cheese
ground pepper
½ cup croutons

Break up lettuce in large wooden bowl. In a smaller wooden bowl, mince anchovies. Use garlic press to mince garlic and add to anchovies. Add remaining ingredients. Pour over lettuce and toss. Top with croutons.

Potato Soup
(serves 12)

4 qt. water
6 potatoes, peeled and finely chopped
¾ cup rice
3 tbsp. butter
1 tbsp. flour
¾ cup sweet cream

Blend butter and flour together, then set aside. To 4 qt. of water, add potatoes and rice. Boil for 1 hour. Add remaining ingredients, including butter, and heat thoroughly, stirring occasionally.

Chuck's Favorite Oatmeal Cookies

¾ cup butter, softened
1 cup dark brown sugar
½ cup granulated sugar
1 egg
¼ cup water
1 tsp. vanilla
1 cup sifted flour
1 tsp. salt
½ tsp. baking soda
3 cups quick oats
1 cup raisins
½ cup chopped walnuts or pecans (optional)

Cream butter and sugars; stir in egg, water, and vanilla. Sift together flour, salt, and soda; add to sugar mixture. Blend in oats, raisins, (and nuts, if desired). Drop by teaspoon onto greased cookie tin and bake at 350° F for 12 to 15 minutes. Cool, remove, and store in a covered container. Yields 5 dozen.

Hamburger Casserole
(serves 6)

8-oz. package elbow macaroni
2 tbsp. butter
1 large onion
1 green pepper
2 lb. ground chuck
salt and pepper
1 cup grated cheddar cheese
2 cans undiluted tomato soup
salt
freshly ground pepper

Cook macaroni according to package directions and drain. Sauté onion and green pepper in butter. Add hamburger and cook until brown. Season with salt and pepper. Place a layer of macaroni and hamburger and alternate with layers of grated cheese. Pour 2 cans undiluted tomato soup over all. Cover and bake in 350° F oven for 45 minutes.

Oyster Fritters
(serves 2–3)

30 stewing oysters
2 eggs
¼ tsp. pepper
¼ tsp. salt
¼ cup + 1 tbsp. flour
1 tsp. baking powder
¼ cup canned evaporated milk or Coffee Rich
oil

Clean the oysters. Drain them in strainer. Beat eggs, add salt and pepper, flour, baking powder, and milk or Coffee Rich. Beat with egg beater. Blend the oysters into this mixture.

Using large Teflon skillet, pour in 1 inch of oil and heat it to 375° F. Drop the mixture by tablespoonful into the hot shortening and fry until brown, turning once. Takes approximately 6 minutes.

Remove and drain on paper towel.

Uncle's Shishkabobs
(serves 6)

Marinade

1 cup olive oil
2 tbsp. fresh lemon juice
2 tbsp. chopped parsley
1 tbsp. salt
2 tsp. oregano
1 tsp. pepper
4 cloves garlic, finely chopped
3 bay leaves

3 lb. boned leg of lamb, cubed
1 onion, quartered
3 green peppers, quartered and seeded
2 tbsp. olive oil
12 slices onion
2 tomatoes, quartered
fresh mushrooms

Marinate lamb cubes overnight in marinade. Sauté green peppers in 2 tbsp. olive oil for 5 minutes. Cool.

Onto six 12″ metal skewers, thread the cubes of lamb, alternating with onion, tomatoes, peppers, and mushrooms. Brush the kabobs with lemon juice and olive oil and broil them 3″ from heat, turning them once, until they are brown on both sides and tender. Also delicious when barbecued. Serve the kabobs with rice.

Damn Good Stew
(serves 6)

2 lb. lean chuck, cubed for stew
2 cans tomatoes, undrained
15-oz. can tomato sauce
½ small onion, sliced
1 cup celery, cut up
6 carrots, cut up
3 potatoes, diced
mushrooms
½ to 1 cup burgundy wine
3 tbsp. Minute Tapioca
1 tbsp. sugar
¾ tbsp. salt
pepper

Mix all ingredients but mushrooms. Cook in 250° F oven, approximately 5½ to 6 hours. Add mushrooms about 20 minutes before finished. Add small amount of sherry if desired.

Chicken Lu Lu
(serves 6)

6 boned chicken breasts
1 can mushroom soup—undiluted
1 cup sour cream
½ lb. fresh mushrooms
⅓ cup sherry

Mix all ingredients and pour over chicken in a glass casserole or large baking dish. Sprinkle with paprika. Bake at 350°F for 1 hour. Serve over Uncle Ben's Long Grain and Wild Rice.

Spinach Soup
(serves 6)

2 packages dry chicken noodle soup
2 packages chopped spinach
2 cups cream sauce

Put in blender to mix thoroughly. Heat for 10 minutes.

Eric's Champagne Cheese Ball

½ lb. sharp cheddar cheese, grated
2 tbsp. butter
6 oz. cream cheese, softened
½ cup champagne (you can use dry white wine if you prefer)
¼ cup finely chopped onion
1 garlic clove, minced
1 tsp. worcestershire sauce
¼ tsp. salt

Topping
1¼ cups chopped walnuts
1 tbsp. chopped parsley
1 tsp. paprika
1 tsp. chili powder
1 tsp. curry powder
1 tsp. dill

In a bowl, combine first three ingredients until thoroughly mixed. Gradually add champagne, stirring all the while. Stir in the onion, garlic, worcestershire sauce, and salt to taste. Cover the mixture and chill for 1 hour.

On a sheet of waxed paper, form the mixture into a ball. In a small dish, combine the topping ingredients. Spread the mixture onto the waxed paper, and roll the ball in it until thoroughly coated. Wrap the ball in fresh waxed paper and chill it for 3 hours or until ready to serve. Serve it with crackers.

J's French Toast
(serves 4)

12 slices white bread
4 large eggs
½ to ⅔ cup milk
pinch of cinnamon
pinch of sugar

Beat eggs well; add milk, cinnamon, and sugar, then beat again. Quickly drop bread into batter, one side at a time. *Do not allow to soak.* Drop on sizzling griddle seasoned with bacon grease. Toast on both sides until golden brown. Serve immediately with butter and Vermont maple syrup and crispy bacon.

For special occasions, serve with powdered sugar and a few drops of bourbon.

THOMPSON–NEELY HOUSE:
Authentic Holiday Celebrations

The Thompson–Neely House at Washington Crossing, Pennsylvania

Colonial holidays were generally festive occasions. Unfortunately, there was one Christmastime that did not lend itself to frivolity. In the year 1776, Washington and his men had camped at Bowman's Hill on the Delaware. Long discussions were undoubtedly held in several of the local homes requisitioned as headquarters for the officers. One of these was the Thompson–Neely House, the river headquarters for Lord Stirling, known as the "House of Decision." During these conversations, the far-reaching decision was made to cross the Delaware and surprise the British and their Hessian allies at Trenton. Historians record that this decision may have won the war.

Our Christmas traditions were most notably influenced by the "Dutch" housewives who introduced dozens of cookies and breads, as well as the favorite holiday fowl: goose. The English were also influential in this respect with their love of good food and drink.

One such favorite recipe (adapted to modern ingredients) follows:

Fruitcake

1 lb. butter
2 cups sugar
½ cup brandy
1 tsp. cinnamon
4 cups sifted all-purpose unbleached flour
9 large egg yolks
7 egg whites
2 cups raisins
2 cups currants
2 oz. citron

Cream butter thoroughly. Gradually add sugar. Add brandy and cinnamon. Add flour, mixing only until blended. Beat yolks and whites together until light and add to batter until all is blended. Fold in raisins, currants, and citron. Pour batter into greased and floured 10″ tube or bundt pan. Bake at 350°F for 1 hour, 15 minutes.

Kitchen of the Thompson–Neely House

51 To Clarrify Butter

of such you will want in Rosting
Take you what quantity you will set in a Sauce pan over a slow
fire & let it boyl a little then let it stand and skum
it clean then pour of clean from the Bottom
& use as occasion serve

52 To Pott Goose or Turkey or both togeł wch is common

Bone ym & season high with pepper salt & a few
Cloves and Bake in a Pan with 2 ℔ of Butter cover the
top with papper or paist and bake 2 hours in a hot
oven or till tender ———— Then take out and press
it well & put it Close in a pot and Cover with the
Clear Fatt and more Clarrifyed Butter ————
If both Goose and Turkey put the Turkey in the
Belly of the Goose and season & bake as before ——
and keep for your use

53 To Pott Chickins or Pullets or Pidgens

Bone and season with salt pepper mace & Cloves but
Pidgens wth salt and pepper only, & bake in a good qty
of Butter till tender n° enough take out press them &
put Close in potts & Cover with the Clear fat mixt with
more Clarrifyed Butter. & keep for Use

Recipes from
Deborah Logan's Cookbook
(Courtesy of Stenton,
Germantown; built in
1723–30 by John Logan)

Pomander balls and
nuts on the table
with pipe, slide rule,
wig curler, and
caliper

A flintlock musket, Brown Bess type, over the fireplace

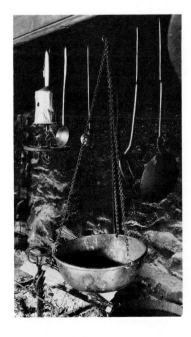

replace and bread oven
the
hompson–Neely kitchen

Here, in the House of Decision, are
quill pens, philosophy book, and spectacles
on the oak table of the Council Room

The barns of the Thompson–Neely estate

St. Valentine's Dinner for Two

CHAMPAGNE COCKTAIL

★ CHICKEN MARTINI

★ CARROT CUTLETS

HEARTS OF PALM SALAD WITH

★ BLEU CHEESE DRESSING

★ STRAWBERRY WHIP

Chicken Martini

1 breast of chicken per person (whole or boned)
1 martini per portion
lemon slices to garnish

Put chicken breasts in baking dish, cover with martinis, then top with lemon slices. Bake at 350° F for 45 minutes.

Carrot Cutlets

½ cup carrots (boiled and mashed)
1 cup boiled rice
½ beaten egg
1½ tsp. canned sweet pepper
1½ tsp. minced onion
1½ tsp. celery salt
1½ tsp. paprika
bread crumbs
1 egg, beaten
currant jelly

Mix first 7 ingredients and form into balls. Flatten them and shape into cutlets. Roll in crumbs, then in egg, and again in crumbs. Sauté or deep fry them in drippings. Place a cube of jelly on each and garnish with parsley.

Bleu Cheese Dressing

1 pt. sour cream
3 tbsp. wine vinegar
½ lb. bleu cheese or Roquefort
½ cup olive oil
white pepper
pinch garlic salt and oregano

Blend all ingredients well. Makes 2 cups.

Strawberry Whip

1 cup strawberries
1 cup granulated sugar
1 egg white
shortcake or angel food cake

Place egg white in bowl and whip until frothy. Add sugar slowly and whip. Add strawberries and whip until peaks form. Serve on slices of angel food cake or shortcake rounds.

Easter Dinner

(serves 6)

★ OYSTERS WRAPPED IN BACON

★ HONEY LAMB

SEASONED RICE

BUTTERED STRINGBEANS

CRESCENT ROLLS

★ SHERRY BUNDT CAKE WITH SHERBET BALLS

★ KATHERINE'S CHOCOLATE EASTER EGGS
(For party favors)

Oysters Wrapped in Bacon

Season large oysters with salt and pepper; cut fat bacon in very thin slices; wrap an oyster in each slice and fasten with a toothpick. Heat a frying pan and add the oysters. Drain on a paper towel after cooking. Place on slices of toast that have been cut into small pieces and serve immediately. Make sure pan is very hot before cooking oysters and watch carefully so they do not burn.

Honey Lamb

7–8 lb. leg of lamb
16-oz. jar honey
6-oz. bottle soya sauce
1 qt. + 1 pt. cold water
garlic

Preheat oven to 250° F. Remove all fat from leg of lamb. Make small cuts on surface of lamb and insert slivers of garlic. Place rack in roasting pan lined with tin foil. Baste with soya sauce and water several times before pouring all of honey over leg of lamb. Put lamb in oven and roast 2½ to 3 hours for rare (longer for well done), basting frequently. If sauce begins to thicken, add more water.

Sherry Bundt Cake

white cake mix
1 small package instant vanilla pudding
4 eggs
⅓ cup (scant) flour
¾ cup oil
¾ cup cream sherry

Combine all ingredients. Beat for 4 minutes in mixer. Bake at 350° F for 40 minutes (for first 15 minutes, cover top with aluminum foil). Cool. Dust top with powdered sugar. Serve with different kinds of sherbet balls rolled in coconut, stacked in pyramid fashion and dribbled with creme de menthe.

Katherine's Chocolate Easter Eggs

three 1-lb. boxes confectioners' sugar
1 cup margarine
2 tsp. vanilla
small amount top milk or half and half
2 packages Bakers semisweet chocolate
2 cans Angel Flake coconut
or:
1 small can crushed pineapple
2 cups chopped walnuts

Mix sugar and margarine until there are no little lumps of margarine, just a fine, crumbly look.

For coconut eggs, mix two cans of coconut with the sugar mixture, then gradually pour in vanilla with the milk until you have a stiff, but not dry, fondant. Knead well. Shape into the size eggs you want, put on a waxed paper lined tray, cover with a towel and refrigerate for several hours. Coat with slowly melted semisweet chocolate (just barely melted in a pan over warm water—it should be of a custard consistency). Spoon the melted chocolate over the bottom of the eggs (which you have turned over). When this is firm, turn eggs over and do the tops on a fresh piece of waxed paper so that any bits from the fondant do not stick to the coating. Cool until firm and wrap in plastic wrap, individually.

Fruit and nut eggs. Drain a can of crushed pineapple in a strainer. Add it to the sugar and margarine mix, a very little at a time. You will find a little pineapple goes a long way. Knead well between additions. When fondant is stiff but not dry, add 2 cups chopped walnuts. Shape and wait. Coat with chocolate in the same manner as coconut eggs.

Memorial Day Luncheon

(serves 6–8)

★ SANGRIA

★ SHRIMP WITH WILD RICE SALAD

★ ASPARAGUS PIE

★ CRUNCHY TOMATO ASPIC

HERB BREAD

★ JEANETTE'S CHEESECAKE

Sangria

2 bottles dry red wine, preferably Spanish red wine
1 cup brandy
two 7-oz. bottles club soda
6 tbsp. lemon juice
6 tbsp. sugar
2 lemons and 2 oranges, sliced paper thin with seeds removed

Put sugar, lemon juice, and fruit into a tall pitcher. Allow to stand 1 hour. Add wine and let stand another 30 minutes to blend all flavors. When ready to serve, add 2 bottles of club soda and plenty of ice and stir. When pouring, give each glass some fruit.

Shrimp with Wild Rice Salad

2 lb. cooked, cleaned shrimp
1½ cups cooked wild rice
½ cup thinly sliced radishes
½ cup chopped celery

Combine all ingredients and chill. Add the following 15 minutes before serving time:

1 pt. favorite French dressing
1 tsp. paprika

1 tbsp. fresh onion juice
dash Tabasco, salt, pepper
½ tsp. curry powder

Garnish the salad with slices of avocado and sliced, peeled tomatoes.

Asparagus Pie

4 lb. fresh asparagus
salt, pepper, and nutmeg or cinnamon, to taste
4½ tbsp. butter
¾ cup grated Gruyère cheese
1 cup shredded proscuitto ham
4–5 eggs, beaten well
4½ tbsp. grated Parmesan cheese

Cook asparagus in salted boiling water until just tender; drain. Cut off tough ends and discard. Cut green portions and tips into 1 to 1½" pieces and return to pan. Sprinkle with salt, pepper, and nutmeg to taste; add butter. When butter has melted, turn into a buttered 9" or 10" pie plate. Sprinkle with Gruyère cheese, cover with proscuitto, and pour beaten eggs over all. Top with Parmesan cheese and bake in preheated 350° F oven 30–40 minutes or until eggs are set and golden crust forms on top.

Crunchy Tomato Aspic

4 cups tomato juice
2 packages lemon jello
⅓ cup chopped celery leaves
⅓ cup chopped onion
1 large bay leaf
4 cloves garlic
3 stalks celery, chopped
1 small can unsalted pecans
1 small jar of large stuffed olives

Soften jello in 1 cup tomato juice. Simmer 2 cups juice with chopped celery leaves, chopped onion, bay leaf, and minced garlic. Strain. Mix softened jello with hot mixture. Stir until jello is thoroughly dissolved. Add remaining tomato juice and refrigerate until thickened. Add chopped celery, pecans, and sliced olives. Pour into lightly greased 2-qt. mold and refrigerate.

Jeanette's Cheesecake

Cookie Dough Crust
- ½ cup flour
- ¼ cup butter or margarine
- ¼ cup sugar
- 1 egg yolk
- 1 tsp. grated lemon rind
- ¼ tsp. vanilla
- 1 tsp. water, if needed

Cheese Filling
- four 8-oz. packages cream cheese
- 1 ⅓ cups sugar
- 1 tbsp. flour
- 1 tbsp. lemon juice
- 1 tsp. grated rind, if desired
- ½ tsp. vanilla
- 5 eggs
- 1 pt. sour cream

Cookie dough crust should be made at least 1 day ahead. Mix all ingredients. Roll out between floured waxed paper, place on bottom section of 9″ spring-form pan. Trim. Bake 12 minutes or until slightly golden at 400° F. Can substitute graham cracker crust.

Cheese Filling

Soften cheese. Gradually beat in sugar and next 4 ingredients. Add eggs, one at a time. Stir in sour cream. Pour filling into crust. Bake at 450° F for 15 minutes, then 250° F for 1 hour. Turn oven off and leave pie in oven, with door open, 1 more hour.

Optional Topping Suggestions

When cool, top with: 1) fresh strawberries and minted strawberry jelly; 2) 1 cup crushed pineapple, thickened with 2 tbsp. cornstarch and 1 tbsp. lemon juice; or 3) in small saucepan, place 2½ tsp. cornstarch and 2 tbsp. sugar, slowly add ¾ cup liquid from canned sour cherries (water packed). Simmer until clear and thick, add ¾ cup cherries, 1 tbsp. lemon juice, and pour over cheese cake.

★ ★

July Fourth Barbecue
(serves 12)

★ AUNT RUBY'S TOMATO COCKTAIL

★ BARBECUED SALMON

BARBECUED CHICKEN

★ COLD VEGETABLE SALAD

★ POTATO SALAD

★ WATERMELON PICKLE

RELISHES

★ SNOWBALL CAKE

★ ★

Aunt Ruby's Tomato Cocktail

4 lb. fresh tomatoes
2 whole onions
1¼ cups oil
¾ cup vinegar
salt and pepper

Peel tomatoes and dice. Score 2 large onions. Combine oil, vinegar, salt, and pepper. Pour over tomatoes and whole onions. Refrigerate and marinate several hours. Remove onions and serve in individual sauce dishes or mugs with assorted crackers.

Barbecued Salmon

Whole salmon, 6–8 lb.
1 large onion, chopped fine
1 cup fresh or frozen lemon juice
1 cup dry white table wine
2 tsp. salt
½ tsp. pepper
1 tsp. thyme

Have salmon cleaned and filleted with skin left on. Marinate both fillets in lemon juice, wine, salt, and pepper for 30 minutes or longer.

Cut a piece of hardware cloth to the size of your grill, or large enough to fit fish, brush it with salad oil and lay salmon on it, skin side down. Spread onion and some of marinade over the top.

Cook over gray coals, with moistened hickory chips added to fire at the beginning and end of cooking. If barbecue has a lid, lower it and leave vent open halfway. If not, make a hood out of foil and place over salmon. Add more marinade near end of cooking. Cook 30–45 minutes. Cover large tray with large leaves, lift hardware cloth with fillets onto tray and serve.

Cold Vegetable Salad

Assorted canned vegetables, such as:
>   lima beans
>   cut green beans
>   whole baby carrots
>   asparagus spears
>   artichoke hearts
>   beets: whole, sliced, or shoestring
>   hearts of palm
>   whole cauliflower

Dressing
>   ½ cup salad or olive oil
>   ½ cup vinegar
>   1 tsp. salt
>   dash black pepper
>   1 small onion, grated
>   2 tbsp. chopped chives
>   2 tbsp. parsley
>   4-oz. can pimento, drained and chopped

Cook whole cauliflower and refrigerate. Mix together dressing ingredients. Put each vegetable in a bowl and pour some dressing over it. Chill several hours or until ready to serve. Arrange vegetables in rows or squares on a platter, with whole cooked cauliflower in center. Pour a little dressing over cauliflower.

Watermelon Pickle

Cut rind into squares and remove all green, leaving a suggestion of pink. Let stand 24 hours in salt water, using about ½ cup of salt to 5 lb. of rind and enough water to cover.

Add a heaping teaspoonful of powdered alum to 2 qt. water. Wash rind and allow to stand in alum water 24 hours or simmer in alum water 30 minutes.

Next, wash well in clean water. Simmer in ginger tea (1 qt. water and 1 tbsp. ginger) until rind looks transparent.

Let cold water run over rind until it is perfectly cold, drain, and put into syrup made as follows: 1 lb. sugar to each lb. rind, dissolve in half and half mixture of vinegar and water (a cup of each to a lb. of sugar), stick of cinnamon broken into pieces (½ oz. to 5 lb. of rind), 5–6 pieces of mace, 1 oz. whole cloves, 1 tbsp. mustard seed, and 1 tsp. celery seed. Boil slowly until the rind is quite clear and shows white spots (about 1½ to 2 hours).

Potato Salad

> 10 potatoes, cooked and cut up
> 10 hard-boiled eggs, cut up
> 2 large onions, diced
> 2 cups Hellmann's mayonnaise
> salt and pepper to taste

Mix ingredients and refrigerate overnight. Garnish with paprika and parsley before serving.

Snowball Cake

> 1 large angel food or chiffon cake
> 4 tbsp. cold water
> 1 tbsp. plain gelatin
> 1 cup boiling water
> dash salt
> 1 cup orange juice
> 1 cup sugar
> 3 tbsp. lemon juice
> 1½ pt. heavy cream, whipped

Soften gelatin in cold water. Add boiling water and mix thoroughly. Add salt, orange juice, sugar, and lemon juice to gelatin mixture. Fold in 1 pt. of the whipped cream. Tear cake into 1″ pieces. Line a large round bowl with waxed paper. Spoon in a layer of the mixture, then a layer of cake. Alternate layers, making sure cake is moistened by the mixture. End with a layer of the mixture. Refrigerate overnight.

Just before serving, turn cake onto a platter, remove waxed paper, and frost with remaining ½ pt. of whipped cream. Decorate with halved cherries or strawberries and blueberries.

Labor Day Buffet

(serves 36)

FRUIT PUNCH

★ CHICKEN CORN SALAD

MARINATED SLICED TOMATOES AND CUCUMBERS

★ HERB-BUTTERED ITALIAN BREAD

★ TINY PECAN TARTS

★ CARROT CAKE

Chicken Corn Salad

12 chicken breasts
6 cups water
6 slices onion
few celery tops
4 tsp. salt
1¼ cups cider vinegar
6 tbsp. sugar
1 tbsp. pepper
3 cups vegetable oil
3 tsp. salt
six 8-oz. packages of small macaroni shells, cooked and drained
six 12-oz. cans of whole kernel corn, well drained
6 cups thinly sliced celery
18 hard-boiled eggs, shelled, coarsely chopped
1½ cups mayonnaise
1¼ tbsp. chopped parsley

Simmer chicken in water with onion, celery, and salt in large, covered saucepan for 30 minutes. Remove and cool chicken. Skin, bone, and cut into bite-size pieces. Combine vinegar, sugar, pepper, and oil in a jar and shake well to mix. Combine macaroni, corn, and celery in a large bowl and mix well with 1¼ cups mayonnaise. Add eggs to chicken, with 6 tbsp. of dressing. Add additional mayonnaise to rest of French dressing and mix with macaroni, celery, and corn. Garnish with parsley.

Herb-Buttered Italian Bread

⅓ lb. butter or margarine
1 tbsp. chopped parsley
1 tbsp. chopped chives
1 tbsp. chopped fresh basil
lemon juice, few drops
whole, unsliced loaf Italian bread

Cream butter until soft; combine with herbs, and add a squeeze of lemon juice to the mixture. After blending, spread thick slices of French or Italian bread which have not been cut quite through the loaf. Butter both sides of slices and wrap loaf in aluminum foil. Heat in 400° F oven for 10 minutes. Also good on pretoasted English muffins. Wrap and heat as directed.

Tiny Pecan Tarts

8 oz. cream cheese
1 cup butter
2 cups flour
2 eggs, slightly beaten
1½ cups light brown sugar
2 tsp. vanilla
½ tsp. salt
2 cups chopped pecans

Blend together soft butter and cream cheese. Stir in flour and make into pastry dough. Divide into 48 balls. Press each ball into tiny muffin pans to form shells.

Combine eggs, sugar, vanilla, and salt and fold into nuts. Fill pastry shells and bake 25–30 minutes, or until filling is set, in 325° F oven. Yield: 48 tarts.

Carrot Cake

2 cups all-purpose flour
2 cups sugar
2 tsp. baking soda
1 tsp. salt
2 tsp. ground cinnamon
4 eggs
1 cup cooking oil
4 cups grated raw carrot (can be done in blender)
½ cup chopped pecans

Sift together flour, sugar, soda, salt, and cinnamon. In large bowl, beat eggs until frothy; slowly beat in oil. Gradually add flour mixture, beating until smooth. Mix in carrots and nuts. Pour into 3 greased and floured 8″ round cake pans. Bake at 350° F for 25–30 minutes, or until done. Cool in pans for 10 minutes and remove. Frost with cream cheese frosting.

Cream Cheese Frosting

4 tbsp. butter or margarine, softened
two 3-oz. packages cream cheese, softened
4⅓ cups powdered sugar
1 tsp. vanilla

Blend butter or margarine and cream cheese. Gradually add powdered sugar, beating until smooth and creamy. Stir in vanilla.

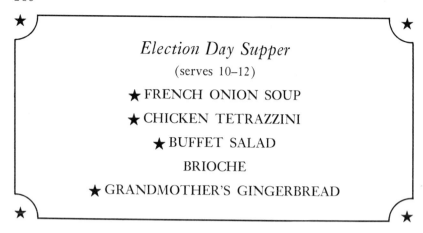

Election Day Supper

(serves 10–12)

★ FRENCH ONION SOUP

★ CHICKEN TETRAZZINI

★ BUFFET SALAD

BRIOCHE

★ GRANDMOTHER'S GINGERBREAD

French Onion Soup

1 clove garlic, mashed
4 large onions, sliced
3 tbsp. bacon drippings
2 tbsp. sugar
2 tbsp. flour
1½ to 2 qt. beef stock
1 cup dry white wine
2 oz. brandy
6 triangles French bread, toasted slowly until crisp
grated Gruyère cheese

Sauté sliced onions and mashed clove of garlic in bacon drippings until brown. Sprinkle with 2 tbsp. of sugar and continue to cook until sugar begins to caramelize. Sprinkle with 2 tbsp. of flour, stir, and then add 1½ to 2 qt. of beef stock. Allow to simmer for about 20 minutes on the edge of the fire, skimming occasionally. Add about 1 cup dry white wine and 2 oz. brandy.

Correct seasoning, pour over toasted triangles in individual oven-proof bowls, cover each triangle with grated Gruyère, and place in hot oven until cheese is well melted. Serve with words of caution so guests don't burn their tongues.

Chicken Tetrazzini

5 or 6 large chicken breasts
1-lb. package thin spaghetti
2 cans mushroom soup
1 soup can milk
2 cans mushrooms or 1 lb. fresh sliced mushrooms, sautéed
    several minutes
3 tbsp. sherry
1 tbsp. worcestershire sauce
½ tsp. each onion and garlic salt
10 oz. sharp cheese, grated
dash pepper and paprika

Cook chicken breasts in water. Remove meat from bones. Cook spaghetti according to directions. In a bowl, mix soup, drained mushrooms, milk, worcestershire sauce, sherry, and salt. Alternate in layers in large casserole: half of spaghetti, half of chicken (boned and cut into large pieces), half of soup mixture, and half of cheese. Add rest of ingredients in same order, ending with cheese. Sprinkle with paprika and pepper. Bake at 350° F, covered, for 30 minutes, then uncovered for additional 30 minutes.

Buffet Salad

1 bunch romaine lettuce
1 head iceberg lettuce
⅓ lb. fresh mushrooms, sliced
1 red onion
1 avocado, diced
2 tomatoes, sliced
⅓ cup Parmesan cheese
½ cup olive oil
¼ cup wine vinegar
garlic salt to taste
pepper

Break up lettuces, add mushrooms, onion, avocado, and tomatoes. Mix oil, vinegar, grated Parmesan cheese, salt, and pepper. Pour on salad and toss.

Grandmother's Gingerbread

½ cup shortening (Crisco)
1 cup dark brown sugar, packed
2 eggs
½ cup barrel molasses
1 tsp. ginger
1 tsp. cinnamon
½ tsp. nutmeg
2 cups flour
1 tsp. baking soda
½ tsp. salt
½ cup boiling water

Place shortening and brown sugar in warm bowl and cream together. Beat in eggs and molasses. Add ginger, cinnamon, nutmeg, and 1 cup flour and beat hard. Add second cup of flour, baking soda, and salt— beat 1 minute by hand. Add boiling water and beat briefly. Bake at 350° F for 30 minutes in 8″ × 12″ pan. (Bread doubles in height while baking.) Serve with lemon sauce.

Lemon Sauce

2 tbsp. cornstarch
½ cup sugar
1 tbsp. butter
1 egg
⅛ tsp. salt
2 cups boiling water
juice and grated rind of 1 lemon

Mix cornstarch and sugar in saucepan. Add butter, egg, and salt. Beat well. Add boiling water slowly and stir over fire until thick. Add lemon juice and rind and remove from fire. Taste and add more lemon juice if needed.

Thanksgiving Dinner
(serves 6–8)

ROAST TURKEY

★ HAAB FAMILY TURKEY STUFFING

★ SWEET POTATO BALLS

★ GREAT GREEN BEANS

★ CRANBERRY SALAD MOLD

CHILLED VEGETABLE TRAY

★ COLE SLAW

★ PUMPKIN MOUSSE

Haab Family Turkey Stuffing

¾ cup chopped onions
2 cups paschal celery
1 package knockwurst
1 loaf white bread (¾ of family size loaf)
poultry seasoning
1 lb. butter

Cut bread into small cubes. Sauté onions and celery. Sauté cubed knockwurst. Sauté bread cubes. Mix everything together. Add poultry seasoning. (The sautéing will use 1 lb. of butter.) This has been the Haab family stuffing for four centuries, originating in Germany. Stuffs one large bird.

Sweet Potato Balls

3 cups hot mashed sweet potatoes
3 tbsp. butter or margarine
⅛ tsp. nutmeg
⅛ tsp. cinnamon
¼ cup brown sugar, or to taste
cornflakes

Mix all ingredients except cereal. Let stand until cool. Mash cornflakes in a bowl. Shape sweet potatoes into balls or croquettes and roll in cornflakes, keeping hands wet. Put on ungreased cookie sheet and bake in moderate oven until brown, 35 minutes at 325° F.

Great Green Beans

two 10-oz. packages frozen French-style green beans, slightly
    undercooked
15-oz. can bean sprouts, drained
8-oz. sliced water chestnuts
½ cup grated Parmesan cheese

Sauce

2 tbsp. butter
2 tbsp. flour
1½ tsp. onion salt
¼ tsp. pepper
dash cayenne
½ tsp. worcestershire
1 pt. light cream

Topping

2 tbsp. melted butter
1 cup chopped almonds

Layer green beans, bean sprouts, water chestnuts, and cheese; coat vegetables with sauce and top with buttered almonds. Bake covered in 1½ qt. casserole 15–20 minutes at 425° F.

Cranberry Salad Mold

3-oz. package cherry or raspberry Jello
8 oz. yogurt (to correspond with Jello flavor)
16-oz. can wholeberry cranberry sauce
small can crushed pineapple
1 cup boiling water
¾ cup cold water

Dissolve Jello in 1 cup boiling water. Add ¾ cup cold water. (The juice of the drained pineapple can be substituted for the cold water, adding water to equal ¾ cup.) Drain pineapple well. Add pineapple, yogurt, and cranberry sauce. Pour into individual molds or a 1-qt. mold. Chill until set.

Cole Slaw

1 head cabbage
1 egg, beaten
⅔ cup sugar (scant)
butter lump, size of egg
½ tsp. mustard
½ cup vinegar

Mix together sauce ingredients and cook until thick. Cabbage should be salted to remove excess water, plunged into ice water, drained dry, and shredded.

Then pour dressing over cabbage, set aside to cool, then refrigerate. When cool, add 1 tbsp. celery seed. Chill.

Pumpkin Mousse

¼ cup + 2 tbsp. applejack
1½ envelopes gelatin
6 eggs
1 cup sugar
1½ cups canned pumpkin
¾ tsp. cinnamon
¾ tsp. ginger
½ tsp. mace
½ tsp. ground cloves
1½ cups heavy cream, whipped
walnut or pecan halves

Form a 2″ collar with oiled waxed paper around a 1-qt. straight-sided soufflé dish. Use rubber band or string to hold in place. Dissolve gelatin in applejack by putting in a small cup set in hot water. Gently fold into whipped cream. In a large bowl, beat eggs until thick and light, about 5 minutes. Gradually beat in sugar. Continue beating for 5 minutes. Add pumpkin and spices; mix thoroughly. Gently fold in whipped cream. Pour into soufflé dish, smooth top and refrigerate 4 hours or more. Decorate top of soufflé with walnut or pecan halves.

Note: If using copper bowl to beat eggs, reduce all amounts by ⅓.

Christmas Dinner
(serves 6)

★ PHEASANT IN WINE

ROAST POTATOES

BRUSSELS SPROUTS

★ SHERRY-CHERRY MOLD

CRESCENT ROLLS IN BUTTER

★ MOCHA-WALNUT TORTE

Pheasant in Wine

2 pheasants
½ cup flour
1½ cups chicken broth
1 tsp. pepper
¼ cup + 2 tbsp. butter
2 tbsp. worcestershire sauce
2 cups wine

Pick, draw, and clean two birds. Cut up as a frying chicken. Combine salt, pepper, and flour in a bag and shake bird pieces until coated. Brown birds quickly in melted butter; add worcestershire sauce, lemon juice, and wine. Cover and place on low heat for about 1 hour, or until tender.

Sherry-Cherry Mold

1-lb. can Bing cherries (drain and reserve liquid)
3-oz. package black cherry gelatin (dissolve in ¾ cup hot water)
½ cup dry sherry
¾ cup cherry syrup
½ cup sour cream
½ cup blanched almonds

Mix gelatin, sherry, and syrup; chill until consistency of unbeaten egg whites. Add cherries, sour cream, and almonds. Pour into 1-qt. mold. Refrigerate and unmold before serving.

Mocha-Walnut Torte

16-oz. package brownie mix
2 eggs
¼ cup water
½ cup coarsely chopped walnuts
2 cups heavy cream
½ cup packed brown sugar
2 tbsp. granulated instant coffee
walnut halves

Stir eggs and water into brownie mix. Add walnuts. Spread into 2 greased 9″ layer cake pans. Bake 20 minutes at 350° F. Turn out to cool.

Whip cream until it begins to thicken. Gradually add brown sugar and coffee. Beat until spreadable. Spread between layers and swirl over top and sides. Garnish with walnut halves. Chill overnight.

★

New Year's Eve Buffet
(serves 8–10)

★ J'S EGG NOG

CHEESE BALL WITH ASSORTED CRACKERS

★ GLAZED BAKED HAM

★ BLACK-EYED PEAS

★ SPINACH AND CABBAGE SALAD

★ PECAN PIE

★ PUMPKIN PIE

★

J's Egg Nog

1½ cups sugar
1 tsp. nutmeg
¾ tsp. salt
5 eggs, beaten
2 tsp. vanilla
½ gal. vanilla ice cream
2 qt. milk
14 oz. rum
6 oz. rye

Rub nutmeg in small portion of sugar to make it fine. Add rest of sugar. Add salt. Add beaten eggs and vanilla to dissolve sugar but *do not whip*. Then, add ice cream, milk, rum, and rye.

Glazed Baked Ham

Glaze for Large Ham
10-oz. jar currant jelly
¼ cup light corn syrup
2–3 tbsp. prepared horseradish
¾ tsp. dry mustard

Combine jelly, syrup, horseradish, and mustard. Stir together and bring to a boil. Baste ham every 10 minutes during last half hour of cooking.

Black-Eyed Peas

    1 package dried black-eyed peas
    1 smoked ham hock
    salt
    pepper

Soak peas in water overnight. The next day, drain, add fresh water, ham hock, and cook until peas are done. These should be eaten after midnight or on New Year's Day to bring good luck for the next year.

Spinach and Cabbage Salad

Dressing
    1 clove garlic, crushed
    1 tbsp. Parmesan cheese
    1 tsp. mustard
    salt and pepper
    1 cup oil
    ½ cup wine vinegar

    1 large package fresh spinach
    1 small head red cabbage
    6–8 slices bacon, cooked and broken
    5–6 hard-boiled eggs, chopped

Mix dressing, prepare greens, and toss.

Pecan Pie

    1 cup dark Karo syrup
    ½ cup sugar
    4 tbsp. butter
    3 eggs
    1 tsp. vanilla
    1 to 1½ cups pecans
    unbaked pie shell

Add sugar to syrup and heat until sugar dissolves. Add butter. Beat eggs and add to syrup with pecans and vanilla. Pour into unbaked pie shell and bake at 450° F for 10 minutes, then reduce heat to 300° F for 30 minutes.

Pumpkin Pie

Filling

   2 cups pumpkin
   ½ cup brown sugar
   ½ cup plain sugar
   3 eggs
   2 cups milk
   ½ tsp. salt
   ¼ tsp. cloves
   ¼ tsp. ginger
   ¼ tsp. nutmeg
   1 tsp. cinnamon

Crust

   ¾ cup butter or margarine
   1½ cups flour

Stir filling ingredients together as listed. Mix well. Pie crust should be made by mixing ¾ cup butter or margarine with 1½ cups flour. Butter should be soft for efficient mixing. Press into pie pan with fingers which have been dipped in flour. Add pumpkin mixture. Bake in 400° F oven for 50 minutes, or until knife comes out clean from center of pie. With this crust, the pie literally melts in your mouth!

Bibliography

Adams, John. *The Adams Papers*, ed. L. H. Butterfield. Series I Diaries; Vol. 2, Diary 1771–1781. Cambridge: Belknap, Harvard U Press, 1961.

Ashmead, Henry Graham. *History of Delaware County, Pennsylvania*. Philadelphia: L. H. Everts & Co., 1884 (Chester: Concord Township Historical Society, John Spenser, 1968).

Bill, Alfred Hoyt. *Valley Forge: The Making of An Army*. New York: Harper, 1952.

Brinton Family Association. *Brinton 1704 House*. West Chester: published for the Brinton Family Association and the Chester County Historical Society, 1959.

Brown, John Hull. *Early American Beverages*. New York: Bonanza Book, 1966.

Chancellor, Paul. *A History of Pottstown, Pennsylvania*. Pottstown: Historical Society of Pottstown, 1953.

Dessert Recipes from Cliveden. Germantown: published for the Cliveden Cookbook Committee (Cliveden is a part of the National Trust for Historic Preservation), 1973.

Dupuy, R. Ernest and Dupuy, Trevor N. *The Compact History of the Revolutionary War*. New York: Hawthorn, 1963.

Earle, Alice Morse. *Child Life in Colonial Days*. New York: Macmillan, 1899, 1966.

Earle, Alice Morse. *Home and Child Life in Colonial Days*, ed. Shirley Glubok. New York: Macmillan, 1969.

Earle, Alice Morse. *Stage-Coach and Tavern Days*. New York: Macmillan, 1900.

Frost, William J. *The Quaker Family in Colonial America*. New York: St. Martin's, 1973.

Futheyand, J. Smith and Cope, Gilbert, *History of Chester County, Pennsylvania*. Philadelphia: L. H. Everts & Co., 1881.

Hutton, Ann Hawkes, *George Washington Crossed Here*. Philadelphia: Franklin Pub., 1966.

Inventory of Historic Sites. Philadelphia: published for the Delaware Valley Regional Planning Commission, 1968.

James, (Mrs.) Thomas Potts. *Memorial of Thomas Potts, Junior*. Cambridge: privately published, 1874.

Kainen, Ruth Cole. *America's Christmas Heritage: Christmas Folklore, Holiday Customs and Recipes from All Over Our Land*. New York: Funk & Wagnall, 1969.

Kimball, Marie. *The Martha Washington Cookbook*. New York: Coward-McCann, 1940.

Lathrop, Elise L. *Early American Inns and Taverns*. New York: McBride & Co., 1926.

Matlack, T. C. *Friends Meeting Houses and the Boarding Homes, Schools and Burial Grounds Associated With Them*, Vol. 10. Moorestown: private papers, 1934.

Peterson, Harold L. *Book of the Continental Soldier*. Harrisburg: Stackpole, 1968.

Project 1776. Pennsylvania Bicentennial Commission, 1973.

Shinn, Henry C. *The History of Mt. Holly*. Mt. Holly: *Mt. Holly Herald*, 1957.

Tannahill, Reay. *Food in History*. New York: Stein and Day, 1973.

Taverns of Yesteryear. Published for Schmidts of Philadelphia, 1960.

From the Files of . . .

Angstadt, Mrs. Edwin C., Jr.

Bevan, Mrs. John S.
Bonar, Mrs. David
Bortle, Mrs. George R. D.
Breish, Mrs. John W., Jr.
Brown, Mrs. Richard A.
Burr, Charles B., II
Burr, Mrs. Charles B., II
Burris, Mrs. Donald D.

Ceasar, Mrs. Albert
Cooper, Mrs. D. Russell, Jr.
Curran, Mrs. William J.

Devoe, Mrs. Stephen J.
Duckett, Mrs. John W.

East, Mrs. William J.
Eckman, Mrs. John W.
Elder, Mrs. Robert M.
Elliott, Mrs. N. Dodson, III

Faragalli, Mrs. Michael
Fernley, Mrs. Thomas A., III
Fiordalis, Mrs. Vincent, II
Ford, Mrs. Leighton B.
Forde, Mrs. David L.
Franks, Mrs. Frederick B., III

Giesa, C. Eric
Giesa, Mrs. C. Eric

Glascock, Mrs. Thomas A., III
Greytok, Mrs. James J.

Haab, Mrs. Frederick C.
Hamilton, Mrs. Wilbur H., Jr.
Hance, Mrs. James H., Jr.
Harley, Mrs. Milton Price
Harrington, Mrs. Chester D., Jr.
Hayward, Mrs. Benjamin Neff
Heckscher, Mrs. Benjamin H.
Helweg, Mrs. Joseph E., Jr.
Henry, Mrs. Richard Lenert
Hollingshead, Mrs. Wickliffe
Hutchinson, Mrs. R. Ford

Joy, Mrs. John Christopher

Kiley, Mrs. Eugene F., III
Krider, Mrs. Harold H., Jr.

Leete, Mrs. William M.

Mallory, Mrs. Paul E.
Marshall, Mrs. James M., III
Mauck, Mrs. Victor, Jr.
McCracken, Mrs. Robert Scott
McKibben, Mrs. Craig L.
Merrill, Mrs. Walter M.
Metts, Mr. William F., Jr.
Mower, Mrs. D. Roger, Jr.

Olson, Mrs. Paul W.

Parker, Mrs. Davis R.
Pattison, J. N., IV
Pattison, Mrs. J. N., IV
Pearcy, George B.
Pearcy, Mrs. George B.
Peck, Mrs. Robert G., III
Peckham, Mrs. George J.
Post, Mrs. Robert Nicholas

Ramsey, Mrs. Peter M.
Rapp, Mrs. William E.
Reichel, Mrs. John, Jr.
Riepe, Mrs. James S.
Rigby, Mrs. Henry Snowden
Rockwell, Mrs. John R.
Rorer, Mrs. Herbert T.
Ross, E. William
Ryan, John E.

Scarlett, Mrs. John A.
Simich, Mrs. Stevan
Simpson, Fred D., Jr.

Simpson, Mrs. Fred D., Jr.
Smedley, Mrs. William, V
Smith, Robert H., Jr.
Smith, Mrs. Robert H., Jr.
Smith, Mrs. Rush B.
Stauffer, William E.
Stauffer, Mrs. William E.
Steel, Mrs. Howard
Stitzer, J. David
Stitzer, Mrs. J. David
Stretch, J. Craig, Jr.

Taylor, Mrs. H. William, III
Tyler, Mrs. R. M., Jr.

Vanderbilt, Mrs. O. DeGray, Jr.

Weary, Mrs. Thomas S.
Widing, Theodore, Jr.
Williams, Mrs. H. Drake, Jr.
Wood, Mrs. Robert B.

Index

Fried Apples and Sausage, 13
Loin of Pork with Glazed Apricots, 134
Pork Chow Mein, 172
Scrapple, 9

VEAL
Veal Scallopini, 121
Veal Stew, 140

MISCELLANEOUS
Creamed Dried Beef, 11
Crêpes, 33
Dutch Egg Pancakes, 13
Haab Family Stuffing, 211
Homemade Crisp Waffles, 10
Joanna's Baked Pineapple, 113
Lunch on an Apple, 53

Pasta

Baked Lasagna, 161

Pies

Caramel Chiffon Pie, 112
Chocolate Pie, 116
Cream Cheese Pie, 168
Festive Apple Pie, 135
Fudge Sundae Pie, 58
Heath Bar Pie, 143
Lemon Cheese Pie, 170
MuMu's Brownie Pie à la Mode, 69
Pecan Pie, 217
Pumpkin Pie, 218
Snowball Pie, 122
Tiny Pecan Tarts, 206

Potatoes and Rice

Linde's Potatoes, 112
Rice Casserole, 121
Rice Timbales, 67
Sweet Potato Balls, 211
Wild Rice and Curried Shrimp, 120

Poultry

Chicken Casserole, 57
Chicken Corn Salad, 205

Chicken Creole, 167
Chicken Curry with Condiments, 125
Chicken in Champagne Sauce, 148
Chicken in Wine, 67
Chicken Livers, 159
Chicken Lu Lu, 185
Chicken Martini, 195
Chicken Sausage Casserole, 117
Chicken Tetrazzini, 209
Creamed Chicken, 27
Easy Chicken Cordon Bleu, 142
Fried Chicken, Cold, 63
Pheasant in Wine, 214
Pollo Alla Florentina, 111

Salad Dressings

Bleu Cheese Dressing, 196
Bonnie's Italian Dressing, 118
French Dressing, 171
Garlic Dressing, 57
Holden's French Dressing, 110
Honey Dressing, 126
Italian Dressing, 133
Russian Dressing, 116
Sis's Salad Dressing, 161

Salads

Buffet Salad, 209
Caesar Salad, 138
Chicken Corn Salad, 205
Chicken Salad, 49
Cold Vegetable Salad, 203
Cole Slaw, 213
Cranberry Salad Mold, 212
Crunchy Tomato Aspic, 200
Cucumber Mousse, 66
Four Bean Salad, 169
French Salad, 137
Grated Carrot Salad, 165
Honeydew Melon Salad, 120
Lime Salad Ring, 49
Marinated Asparagus Mold, 114
Molded Salmon Salad, 55
Pam's Italian Tomatoes, 111
Potato Salad, 204
Sherry Cherry Mold, 214
Shrimp and Wild Rice Salad, 199
Simpson's Caesar Salad, 181
Spinach and Cabbage Salad, 217

2913 1